CON(

CONCILIUM

ADVISORY COMMITTEE

CONCILIUM 2021/1

Church and Theology at the Borders

Edited by

Gianluca Montaldi,
Catherine Cornille and Daniel Franklin Pilario

Published in 2021 by SCM Press, 3rd Floor, Invicta House, 108–114 Golden Lane,
London EC1Y 0TG.

SCM Press is an imprint of Hymns Ancient & Modern Ltd (a registered charity)
13A Hellesdon Park Road, Norwich NR6 5DR, UK

ISBN 978-0-334-03157-4

Printed in the UK by
Ashford, Hampshire

Concilium is published in March, June, August, October, December

Contents

Editorial

Whether implicitly or explicitly, borders have always harboured profound theological meaning. The border is, on the one hand, an instrument to establish an identity by demarcating oneself from others, but, on the other hand, it can also be experienced as a possibility of exchange. From an anthropological point of view, it is both a limitation and a starting point. Because of this ambiguity, particular attention must be paid to the fragility of those who live "on the margins", or "in magical territories" (Gloria Andalzúa). Moreover, in our time, we observe a profound change in the existential experience of the "border". The reasons are many: problems related to climate change, access to clean water and air, differences in development and economic and financial resources, political instability and violence are pushing more and more people around the world to cross borders. This crossing could be the figure of a new humanity and a new cohabitation, in which the religious and spiritual resources of each person and each group can have their own role. As a result, theology is deeply involved in this reflection, but it must engage in dialogue with other disciplines.

The annual *Concilium* meeting was to be celebrated in 2020 in Palermo, Italy, in collaboration with the Theological Faculty of Palermo and SIRT (Società Italiana per la Ricerca Teologica). As always, reality is stronger than ideas, and this time it presented itself in the form of an invisible biological force that disrupted the larger projects. We had to change plans for our yearly meeting, but still wanted to maintain the focus of the conference on the topic:"Borders: a Mediterranean way". The location of the conference in Palermo and Sicily would have allowed to place these reflections in a precise historical, geographical and cultural context, a marginal territory in itself, formed by the encounters between different religions and cultures. The goal was thus to start a dialogue on the meaning of living "on the margins". This explains why many of the contributions in this volume come from Italy and southern Europe and why we focus on the

Mediterranean. These areas are doubly marginal to Europe and the world (and their respective theologies). It represents as a laboratory from which to reflect on the function and on the challenges of borders. The dramatic events unfolding on the visible and invisible Mediterranean borders thus offers an important "locus" to reflect on the broader theological meaning of borders.

In such areas, it is evident that one cannot escape from borders but one must find a way to live within them, implementing forms of human resilience. The texts of the first part of the volume starts suggesting the possibility of forms of evangelical coexistence at the borders of a city like Palermo, that is in the world of the suburbs (Anna Staropoli). But, on the contrary, there is always a possibility to strengthen borders. Hence the importance of 'deconstructing' them, whether this involves overcoming the frontiers between nature and technique (Giovanni Giorgio) or rising beyond the borders that separate different cultures and peoples (Sharon A. Bong, Carlos Mendoza Alvarez). In his concluding article, Stan Chu Ilo reflects on how theology should allow itself to be questioned and changed by the contemporary realities of border building and border crossing.

Since the European project was also born from a desire to loosen borders, the second part of this volume deals with continuing challenges of European integration and its own relation to "the stranger" (Michelle Becka, Johannes Ulrich, Cettina Militello, Zoran Grozdanov), with a special look at its southern border (Valerio Corradi, Giuseppina de Simone). The dense final text suggests, in the way of an epilogue, the possibility of applying this reflection also in art, with a brief theological commentary on the mosaics of the Palatine Chapel in Palermo, where East and West meet in an almost natural way.

The forum presents two reflections that critically deal with the pandemic situation, one from a philosophical point of view (Kristoff Vanhoutte) and one from a liturgical perspective (Alberto dal Maso).

Gianluca Montaldi, Catherine Cornille and Daniel Franklin Pilario

Part One: A Global Vision

The Peripheries of Waste: Touchstone and Opening Towards Infinity

ANNA STAROPOLI

The vulnerable *are the meeting ground between social and political, they are the touchstone: our hopes for change are linked to our ability to re-orient the political imaginary in which we are immersed for the construction of meaningful social bonds. We need a transformative political practice that can be* transgressive, disarmed *and* vulnerable; *that is capable of being surprised by the new that is emerging; that accompanies the processes of community growth towards autonomy, leaving the weapons of stereotypes, ideologies and prejudices; that is capable of crossing collective wounds and transforming them into opportunities for personal and community growth. The educational vision that seems to me useful to propose is that of a dreamy pedagogy, not only a social or urban one. Community participation can become, in fact, the pedagogical* setting *in which to re-establish links and mature sharing: a fertile ground from which democracy can find meaning to re-energize itself.*

The hell of the living beings is not something that will be in the future; if there is one, it is what is already here, the hell that we live every day, that we form together. There are two ways not to suffer from it. The first is easy for many: accept hell and become part of it to the point of no longer seeing it. The second is risky and requires continuous attention and learning: to seek and recognize who and what, in the midst of hell, is not hell, and make it last, and give it space.
Italo Calvino, *Invisible Cities.*

11

A new humanism can be born from a reflection on the city that chooses an approach *from below* and *from within* the city communities, embodied in the *crossroads* of history, in the turning points that today are precisely *the non-places* of politics, the places of *marginality*, *the stone discarded by the builders that has become a cornerstone* where something unexpected, unforeseen is being born: the existential and social peripheries.

The *vulnerable* are the meeting ground between social and political, they are the *touchstones*: our hopes for change are linked to our ability to re-orient the political imaginary in which we are immersed for the construction of meaningful social bonds.

I The peripheries of waste and global citizenship

The *bankruptcy of humanity*, the result of economic imperialism and the cultural globalization of neo-liberalism has produced waste, physical and human waste. The destination of waste is the landfill, the human garbage dump. "We dispose of leftovers in the most radical and efficient way: we make them invisible by not looking at them, and unthinkable by not thinking about them".[1] The boundary is the difference between the admitted and the rejected, between the included and the excluded.

The Mediterranean, the new *Lake of Tiberias*,[2] *returning us pieces of boat that have become "sacred", will always remind us that together with the many lifeless bodies that are in its depths, there is also the dream of a welcoming and supportive Europe sacrificed on the altar of economic and political interests.*

Even in our cities there are the "non-places" of humanity, the no-man's-lands. The anthropologist Ferdinando Fava defines them as "*off-limits* places", represented and maintained as such; those who inhabit them carry the signs of the stigma in their bodies and in the cement, a stigma that is imprinted as stigmata in their lives and in their homes. "They were implanted at the borders of the urban world and for this reason they are also *eschata* (a New Testament category that contains both a spatial and temporal dimension): they are not last places but also 'last placed', 'extreme terms'".[3]

They are apocalyptic places, places of discernment, which, lifting the veil of appearances, reveal to us the political-economic order that governs the whole city, but also the new one that is being born. The territorial context is not only a passive background, it is not a neutral scenario, but becomes the central actor of the city and "puts us to the test", as a place where life stories are generated. In this way a twofold transformative movement is realized: on the one hand the possibility to cross contexts, to trace their boundaries, to smell their scents and perfumes, to know their hidden undertones, to listen to the voices of those who live there, to recognize their looks opening to diversity; on the other hand, an inner movement, to let oneself be crossed by contexts, which transform our interpretative categories, our way of being in the world.

Often those who remain mute do so because the world around them never questions them and never gives them the opportunity to express thoughts and words. In social work it is necessary to activate transformative processes to make the mute speak, to recognize citizenship to those who live on the margins. Political formation can no longer be understood as the formation of an "elite" leadership, of a restricted elite, that decides in representation, on behalf of and in the name of others, but must become training for a "widespread" leadership in the territory, capable of generating other leaders.

The leader is first and foremost *auctor*, that is, the one who 'promotes', who takes an initiative, who is the first to produce an activity that inevitably bears the imprint of the singularity that originated it: "the leader is the one who, having recognized himself as an author, allows others to become one".[4] To acknowledge the subjectivity of people and communities it is necessary to break the vicious circle of self-reproducing marginality, recognizing the possibility of transforming conflicts from stories of tragedy, subjection and wounds into stories of dignity, courage and public happiness.

II The transformation of conflicts: the two symbols of door and square

Democracy is not only a system of rules. It is the deposit of non-violent conflict management practices in the collective memory. It must be nurtured and taken care of so that it can regenerate itself. To open the sacred tabernacle of our humanity means to be able to recognize oneself in the fragility, in the best and the worst of each one of us, to give a name to the emotions, to the wounds that burn bleeding in the living flesh and desire to be crossed and transformed in order to give oneself peace. The encounter of different histories and cultures can be represented by two symbols: the *door* and the *square*.

The door is a symbol that helps to develop many reflections. It is time to take steps. It is the new times that demand a cultural change.

> "From the dungeons of history come burning questions, the dungeons of history are the poor, those who have no power, who count for nothing. Those who too often serve to confirm our ideological apparatus or to accredit us in our goodness. But these situations should dismantle any accreditation and fill us with a lot of doubts, questions, anxieties...".[5]

Real exclusive democracies with persistent inequalities: a minefield in which the war of all against all can break out at any moment. We need a border policy that knows how to stand at the door, that knows how to grasp the signs of the times through a communal gaze and discernment: "what" the last places in the cities and the outskirts of the world reveal?

The *square*, the *agora*, is a place of exchange and creative connections for parts of the cities that are difficult to meet, inviting them to leave their self-referential worlds, towards cosmopolitan cities: to offer a "square", a place of truth and freedom, where they can recognize each other as people and as a community, giving back subjectivity, desires and originality. We need to generate a culture of community, a massive approach to homes to reassure and explore, understand problems and inventions that only the monotonous trampling of everyday life can reveal to us: "It's as if a setting had to be given to hope, to the thinkability of the future".[6]

It is therefore prophetic to be able to bet on what few have had the courage to invest in these decades: the collective intelligence of ordinary people, the intelligence of everyday life at work, the wisdom of the experience of the worlds of life. We must recognize it, value it, connect it.

III Case studies of community conflict mediation in Palermo: the second-hand market in Albergheria and the rural district of Danisinni[7]

The community mediation of conflicts has the advantage of proximity, respect and recognition of all those involved, so that they can exercise a responsible, cooperative and supportive self-assessment of their conflicts.

14

It is a matter of generating empathic micro-communities as areas of ethical life and construction of meaning, a movement of participation that promotes the awareness of being a resource as a community, generating relationality, self-reflexivity and co-authorship. No one is so poor that they cannot give something and so rich that they cannot receive it.

At the Albergheria, a neighbourhood in the historic centre of Palermo, a second-hand market has come to life that allows everyone not to forget and not to leave many marginal lives in oblivion, as a social challenge and amplified communication of a malaise that does not give up and wants to turn into well-being or rather as the good to be, to exist. I returned to the Albergheria after several years and I feel at home here, where I grew up and became confronted with the citizenship system and its mechanisms of exclusion, opening myself to sociological reflections and instances of social justice: I learned from the Albergheria to be a citizen of Palermo and to love this city.

With the Community Conflict Mediation Group, promoted by the Office of Mediations and Restorative Justice of the Municipality of Palermo, we decided an initial activity to raise awareness and listen to the desires and experiences of the market by the people who live and work in it, to listen to the many truths and the many reasons related to that neighbourhood by those who live it daily, feeling that it is a public space of sharing and conflict, meeting and confrontation but often also a projection of the private space.

All the stereotypes and prejudices heard on the second-hand market collapsed when I heard the emotions, life experiences, stories of the many people I met: the lady sitting in front of the council houses laughing and having fun talking to us with the confidence of those who feel they have the history of the neighbourhood in their hands; the grandson who runs a small grocery store and is a point of reference for street vendors; families with children sleeping in the street or in the car to ensure a good location for the market.

Beside a concrete solidarity made of simple and authentic gestures, there is also the inner conflict of some residents who look out onto the balcony to tell contrasting emotions: on the one hand, they feel the weight, anger, rancour and fatigue of the disturbed nights and the awakenings at dawn by the noises and screamed voices of the "mercatari" [merchants] fighting over a place, the goods on the ground cluttering the sidewalks and the street blocking the doors and exits of buildings and schools, the waste of unsold clothes and shoes and bulky objects, nets, pieces of household appliances. On the other hand, they feel emotion and respect for those family fathers who make a living expressing dismay, a sense of injustice and solidarity for a poverty that must be content to make use of the waste of others. We feel the full weight of this responsibility and these expectations. There is a strong desire in us to tiptoe, not promising what we cannot give and to build together in small steps a possibility of transformation of conflicts into opportunities for meeting and listening to each other.

The market is the impossible that becomes possible, a tower of Babel, many languages and many diversities that mingle and find a precarious balance to feel like a community, a common challenge to poverty and the fragility of their lives: some found themselves there after a marriage separation, some after traveling the world with the most varied jobs, some after a wrong experience for some crime committed, some lost their jobs and found themselves in difficult economic situations and homelessness, some come from other countries and Roma communities and find in the informality of the market a chance of survival. The market has given dignity to many people and has filled their days with meaning, restoring a rhythm to everyday life.

Among the historical *mercatari*, among the first people met were Giovanni, the mayor, as he calls himself, who is also a poet, and Grazia who is the wise person in the community who knows how to listen and weave the bonds between the *mercatari*. They gained a sense of identity and belonging to the market that gave them the opportunity to be seen and recognized, defeating loneliness and weaving new friendships.

There is not just one market but many markets in the Albergheria which is a complex microcosm where entire families who have lived there for several generations and who share the activity as a sort of small business for family survival are involved. There is a midweek market and one on the weekends, made by merchants who come from other neighbourhoods and neighbouring municipalities; in the last, the type of goods is more bulky and it often comes into conflict with the stable market and residents.

A market of illegality also crosses it with some critical issues that weigh on the people who live and work in the neighbourhood. Also, the need for an exchange and a virtuous circle between the historic market of Ballarò and the second-hand market of Albergheria is emerging through the activation of a regulatory process.

The collaboration with the Office of mediation and restorative justice of the Municipality of Palermo allowed me to participate in another experimentation of community mediation: a training course as community mediators of some women of the Danisinni district of Palermo. It is a rural village with a vegetable garden and a social farm, so close to the heart of the city, to the palaces of power, from the seat of the Parliament of the Sicilian Region to the City Hall of the Municipality of Palermo, and at the same time so far and marginal with respect to the distribution of socio-economic, political and cultural resources.

It is a small country village with a square populated by children: children running, chasing each other, adult children holding other children in their arms. Voices of mothers speaking to themselves at the windows resting on the balcony with the weight of life on them. Voices of men from the taverns, tireless seekers of a desired, lost or never found work. Strands of coloured clothes of all sizes and, in the centre of the imposing square almost to occupy it all, a former kindergarten, abandoned building marked by time. So many invisible cities that sometimes mix and merge and sometimes live independently each with a life of their own.

Among the many, there is the green city of the garden, full of aubergine and fresh tomatoes, which smells of lavender and orange blossom, announcing the spring of life. It has a gardener with a beautiful story behind him who revived the plants, sowed hope, in a dry soil and so his life has flourished again free from the past of prison, a full life, crossed by the pain and joy of the harvest.

There is the city of prayer and sacred feasts of St. Agnes parish, guardian of history and traditions, which has sustained the hunger and thirst of the community in difficult times. It has lit a light for the whole city in the living nativity scene that that village represents. Here come the Three Kings with gifts of wisdom and beauty but also some, like King Herod, ready to exploit the poverty of others. "Make way for the poor without making way", said Don Milani.

The city of the square, the city of men and the city of women, the wine to forget and the smell of the kitchens to feel alive. Rites of many cities where black and white are mixed with the colours of the rainbow, as many shades as the lives that inhabit the square, strong colours that the harshness of existence has invented. Short films and fragments of truth, shards to be joined, where the smile comes out together with a tear. Stories of women who for the love of their children are ready to challenge the world, alone against the judgments that weigh on them, but strong with the love of the child, who is son and father, hope and pain. The city of children, noisy children who populate the streets, fast brushstrokes of an impressionist painting, children always on the move like life. Little travellers without a route, overwhelmed by the strongest current, hold their dreams to their chests.

The community mediation of conflicts and the training of some women in the neighbourhood as equal mediators, territorial antennae that have the opportunity to bring out conflicts, wounded humanity, has created an authentic meeting place without judgment to create new words, a new collective narrative: words that generate other words in the game of life.

IV Conclusions: Dreamy pedagogy

The *dreamy pedagogy* recovers the dimension of desire, reinterprets it and makes it a shared project. It was useful for me to use the Ignatian pedagogical paradigm: context-experience-reflection-action-evaluation, applying it to the social reality of the different experiences observed in order to move towards political choices capable of being "contemplative in action":

Context: Starting from the context is to recognize the diversity and uniqueness of the social experience that is never the same and is built from the concrete people involved and their life and social contexts. The urban space "summons us" and "puts us to the test" in the crossroads of history, in the non-places of politics: migrants, social and existential peripheries, young people.

Experience: The experience, the narration of the experience, the meeting allows us to overcome the pre-comprehensions dictated by roles, stereotypes, and to go beyond stigmatizations. How to make the recipient, the object of the action also the subject of action, co-author and protagonist. The *surprise* of some experiences or of some territorial encounters disorient us and open us to the unexpected, putting us in crisis and setting something new in motion in us.

Reflection: Reflection can be stimulated by a constant attitude of *researching those who participate* and, as *researchers*, being interested in what you do not see, what is not yet, in the discovery of new things. Reflection acts through a constant attitude of re-reading and accompanying experiences. *What new developments of reflection were born through experiences? What phases of development? What are the blocks? The steps forward?*

Action: Social processes and authentic networks must be accompanied so that the new that is born and social practices do not die. Therefore we choose to be inside the processes and within the territories through an approach "from the inside and from below" and not "from the outside and from above".

Evaluation: Evaluating a generative action allows us to always return to the *deep sense* of what originated it. It is an *acted reflection* that in the perspective of circularity has chosen to consider the city as an educating community as a whole, involving as *empathic micro-communities* different neighbourhoods of the suburbs and the historic centre and the actors who live and love there.

The educational vision that seems useful to me to propose is that of a "dreamy pedagogy", and not only social or urban.[8] Community participation can become, in fact, the pedagogical setting in which to learn relationships, re-establish ties and mature sharing, where one can experience a sense of belonging against exasperated individualism: a fertile ground from which democracy can find meaning to re-generate itself.

In the encyclical *Fratelli Tutti* (*Brothers All*) (of October 3, 2020), as he had already done in the document *Querida Amazzonia*, Pope Francis uses dreamy pedagogy as a chance to revive a worldwide aspiration to universal brotherhood and social friendship: "We dream as one humanity, as wayfarers made of the same human flesh, as children of this same land that is home to all of us, each with the richness of his/her faith or convictions, each with his/her own voice, all brothers!"[9]

Notes

1. Zygmunt Bauman, "Vite di scarto", Bari: Editori La Terza, 2019, 35.
2. Today we could collect Giorgio La Pira's dream "to make the Mediterranean the new Lake of Tiberias (...) a potential symbol of peace for all continents through the rediscovery of the one God who unites the family of Abraham (Jews, Christians, Muslims)": Andrea Nastasii, "Mediterraneo: Ipotesi di futuri scenari", in "Spes contra Spem: Atti del IV Convegno nazionale Giorgio La Pira", Palermo 13-14 ottobre 2017, Firenze: Edizioni Polistampa, 2018, 150.
3. Ferdinando Fava, "In ascolto degli 'ultimi posti' della città", Aggiornamenti Sociali, anno 67/1 (2016), 51-61, qui 58.
4. Ferdinando Fava, *Formare alla leadership L'accesso all'originalità personale*, Aggiornamenti Sociali 12 (2003), Milano: Fondazione Culturale San Fedele, Milano, 175-800, qui 800.
5. Roberto Camarlinghi, Francesco d'Angella, Franco Floris, "Per una costituente del lavoro sociale ed educativo: Ritornare nei territori", Animazione Sociale, Torino: Edizioni Gruppo Abele, 338 (2015), 1-13, here 12, at http://www.animazionesociale.it/wp-content/uploads/2015/12/Per-una-costituente.pdf.
6. Gino Mazzoli, "Spunti per dare un setting alla speranza: Le competenze per il lavoro socio-politico", in Gino Mazzoli (edds.) "Costruire partecipazione nel tempo della vulnerabilità", Animazione Sociale, Supplemento 259 (2012), Torino: Edizioni Gruppo Abele, 39-47, qui 40.
7. These case-studies, life stories and testimonies have been reworked by the undersigned within the thesis (under discussion) on "Community mediation of conflicts" for the Training Course for Social and Criminal Mediators, restorative justice operators, promoted by the Spondè Association and collected through direct listening and field experimentation in collaboration with the activities promoted by the Operative Unity "Mediations and restorative justice" of the Municipality of Palermo.
8. Ezio Del Gottardo, Comunità educante, apprendimento esperienziale, comunità competente, Napoli: Giapeto Editore , 2016, 100.
9. Lettera Enciclica del Santo Padre Francesco, "Fratelli Tutti: Sulla fraternità e l'amicizia sociale", 3 ottobre 2020, a http://www.vatican.va/content/francesco/it/encyclicals/documents/papa-francesco_20201003_enciclica-fratelli-tutti.html/ [12 Ottobre 2020], Senza Frontiere, 8.

Encountering the Stranger at the Gate: Towards a Feminist-Postcolonial Theology of Hospitality

SHARON A BONG

This paper asks: Who is the stranger? Who defines this and for whom? How do we encounter the stranger? I begin by tracing Malaysia's treatment of refugees, as paradigmatic of the marginalised, in the time of coronavirus when the Government of Malaysia had imposed a partial lockdown from March to September 2020. A cursory scoping of headlines during this period not only answers those questions but is also revelatory of the shifts in mind-sets and treatment of refugees in Malaysia; one from civility to hostility. I contrast that with my personal encounter with refugee female leaders. And I offer a theology of hospitality from a feminist-postcolonial lens borne from this encounter of difference, mutuality and reciprocity.

Who is the stranger? Who defines this and for whom? How do we encounter the stranger? I begin with the treatment of refugees in the time of coronavirus in Malaysia and contrast that with my personal encounter with refugee female leaders. And I offer a theology of hospitality from a feminist-postcolonial lens borne from this encounter of difference, mutuality and reciprocity.

A cursory scoping of news reports in the time of coronavirus related to Malaysia's treatment of refugees, as paradigmatic of the marginalised is revelatory of the shifts in mind-sets and treatment of refugees in Malaysia. The Government of Malaysia (GoM) first received commendation by the UNHCR-Malaysia, the UN Refugee Agency in Malaysia, as it assured refugees who came forward to be tested that they would not be arrested or deported (there are approximately 180 000 registered refugees with the

21

UNHCR-Malaysia).[1] But on the pretext of managing the rise of infections during the first phase of the MCO, police raided the mainly inhospitable dwellings of migrant workers, many of whom are undocumented and detained them. With the spike in infections at immigration detention centres, many Malaysians, spooked by daily reports of climbing figures and its clusters, directed their anxieties at 'the (poor) foreigner' as vectors of disease of a life-threatening virus and they were scapegoated by hate speeches across social media platforms with netizens divided over their perception and treatment of non-citizens.[2] In managing the pandemic, national borders were more stringently policed with the GoM maintaining its stance, despite criticism by local and global human rights advocates, of pushing back Rohingya asylum seekers arriving in boats fleeing religious persecution. Approximately 101,000 Rohingya refugees have found refuge in Malaysia.

As a Malaysian, I was saddened at times at the vitriol directed at the marginalised, who are triply burdened on account of their statelessness, poverty, and vulnerability to multi-faceted violence by citizens who are mostly more privileged albeit differently impacted by the pandemic. Refugees at the figurative gate or literal waters waiting to be welcomed are emblematic of 'the stranger' as they embody precarity by inhabiting the borders of inside/outside, citizen/alien, and purity/pollution. Refugees as the unwelcomed guest are also at the mercy of inhospitable hosts; they are an outcast people with some belittling them – along with migrant workers who handle the 'three "D jobs" (dirty, demanding and dangerous)' that Malaysians will not take on – with the 'three "D stigmas" (disease, depravity and drugs)'.[3] Others who are conscientised about social justice, initiated hashtag movements such as #migrantsarehuman and #nohumanisillegal.

Strangers are not only encountered at the borders, as evidenced by the lived realities of survivors of sexual-and-gender-based violence (SGBV) experienced at home among familial members and LGBT Malaysians made lesser citizens in their home country.[4] 'Home' thus de-romanticised as a place of refuge for all at all times becomes a trope of differentiation, delimitation and denunciation that is predicated on sexism, heterosexism, homophobia, transphobia, racism and xenophobia. This is not our (Covid-19-driven) new normal but rather old normal.

But there are other ways to encounter the stranger, essentially, for strangers to encounter each other. And I was privileged to have had this experience when I agreed to facilitate a series of gender and development awareness training for stakeholders that included refugee female leaders, refugee male leaders and UNHCR and partner staff from October to November 2018, a time before coronavirus. The training aimed to enable gender mainstreaming across all UNHCR operations and programmes, as a coordinated and multi-sectoral approach envisioned by the *UNHCR 2018 Policy on Age, Gender, and Diversity* on institutionalising respect for diversity and inclusion.[5] The refugee female and male leaders whom I had encountered carry the UN card (signifying their refugee status) with many awaiting resettlement to third countries (when asked, these vary from Australia to the UK, even Switzerland). I recall making the quip that no one wants to live in Malaysia; it is appreciated mainly as a host country rather than a destination or third country. And what a poor host it turned out to be in the time of coronavirus! As the GoM is not a signatory of the 1951 Refugee Convention and its 1967 Protocol, there are no formal mechanisms in place – legislative or administrative – to offer adequate protection to asylum-seekers and refugees in Malaysia. The UNHCR Malaysia, itself resting literally on precarious grounds as it is not officially registered, performs this integral albeit intermediary role of overseeing the reception, registration, documentation and refugee status determination of asylum-seekers and refugees.

This shelter in the form of the UNHCR, has two gates; one for asylum-seekers and refugees, and the other, for others (e.g. staff and visitors). Situated next to an army barracks, I waited alone at the security guardhouse to have my identity processed and looked across at the queue of asylum-seekers and refugees also waiting to have their identities processed. I was warmly received by one of the staff of the Community-based unit, a former student whose passion in Gender Studies equals mine. Although the UN representation in Malaysia began in 1975 (when the two-decade Vietnam war between North and South Vietnam ended), with Vietnamese refugees who arrived by boat,[6] this is the first time, more than four decades later, that I had set foot at the UNHCR. *I was the stranger*. When I was ushered to the meeting room where the refugee female leaders were already assembled and waiting (with some having travelled for hours to this location in Kuala

Lumpur), my sense of strangeness as the outsider increased, given that the UNHCR is both a familiar and, to some extent, familial space to everyone else gathered. With at least fifteen pairs of eyes staring at me, undoubtedly appraising my credentials as 'the expert' in standing before them, I took a deep breath and... invited them to guess my age (a preoccupation with most women)! The tension immediately eased as smiles and giggles broke out and one woman, a Somalian refugee, correctly guessed my age.

There was a total of 15 refugee female leaders with ages ranging from twenty-something to fifty-something and they hail from countries of origin such as: Myanmar in Southeast Asia, Sri Lanka and Pakistan in South Asia, Afghanistan, Iran and Somalia. Participants also included three very enthusiastic interpreters for whom operationalising a gender perspective in their everyday operations at the UNHCR was still a novelty. I started the two-day workshop with 'Our stories' aimed at exploring our diverse and shared experiences. This activity entailed a woman standing and naming a category that she belongs to and others in the same category choosing to stand with her (or not). Some of the categories called out by the refugee female leaders, in the order of most commonly to least commonly shared, include: 'woman', 'living in Malaysia', 'refugee' (my former student and I were the minority for this category), 'faced so many difficult hazards in my life', 'I am a girl and I love my siblings', 'feminist' and 'woman who shuts people out to enjoy my own space' (categories which 50 percent identified with), 'mother', 'do not support LGBT but will not judge them', and 'I am a woman who wants to dominate over men' (meaning stand up for her rights). I noted with interest that when this activity was replicated (a month later) in a mixed group comprising refugee male and female leaders, the men named mostly physical or apparent differences, e.g. 'community leaders', 'black hair', 'two eyes', 'wears glasses', 'Muslim', 'Arab', etc.

Another noteworthy activity on day 1 was creating a 'Web of equality'. The activity aims to enable women to recall and analyse personal experiences of self-assertion. The telling of their stories included prompts such as: where did this event occur, why did you assert your rights, how did you feel before, during and after, was this experience in the home or outside the home, how did people react or respond, were you supported, and what where the consequences of your action. The analysis of their stories included prompts such as: who or what helped you to stand up for yourself, what aspects of your personality led to your action, did you have the support of other women or men, did you have role models of other women, did your education enable your action, did community tradition support your action, and what are conditions necessary for women to recognise their needs and stand up for themselves? The activity culminated in participants drawing a 'Web of equality' in identifying 'acts of self-assertion' (e.g. saying no to an arranged marriage, insisting on her right to basic education) and 'factors that helped' (e.g. parental rather than community support, in particular, mothers).

Having introduced and explained concepts such as gender binaries (e.g. male/female, masculine/feminine), how gender equality (equality as sameness) is different from gender equity (equality as difference as women are differently and disproportionately affected), we moved onto more sensitive and potentially traumatising issues related to SGBV as well as women's human rights on day 2. The participants were invited to create vignettes comprising their lived realities as well as that of other refugee women known to them. Many could identify with this vignette:

A young woman refugee arrives at a camp without her family. In order to get enough food, she accepts an offer made by a guard to get her a 'good job'. Instead of a good job, she finds herself working in a brothel where she isn't allowed to keep her wages. She can't complain to the police because they are part of the racket. Most customers refuse to wear condoms. Soon, she contracts a sexually transmitted illness (STI).

They shared deeply articulating first-hand experiences of hopelessness and resilience. This activity culminated in a role play aimed at understanding why some women find it difficult to leave a situation of violence (e.g. dependency on husbands, lack of community or familial support) and identify opportunities that might support their leaving (e.g. when women have power outside the home, when the community acts to stop SGBV, and when women unite).

Who is the stranger? Who defines this and for whom? Derrida speaks of a 'radical hospitality' that '*would have* to consist, in receiving without invitation, beyond or before the invitation'. By this, he suggests on the one hand, that hospitality is 'culture itself' in the perpetual preparedness of the host to welcome the stranger, the foreigner ('*l'etranger*'). In an Asian-Malaysian context, this holds true: that hospitality is a quintessential way of life or 'culture itself'. 'But, *on the other hand*', Derrida adds, 'to be hospitable is to let oneself be overtaken…to *be ready to not be ready*', even at risk of being violated by a hostile stranger.[7] Many feed the hungry or clothe the naked even though they are poor and almost overtaken by hardships in this pandemic – amid the three D new normal – despair, drudgery and death.

Yet from a feminist perspective, such a masculinist interpretive offer of hospitality, is objectionable as it abstracts and trivialises the lived experiences of many women, including refugees who are 'violated and raped' not only by hostile strangers but also those known to them. It is also problematic from a feminist-postcolonial perspective, as a culture steeped in 'Asian values'[8] and mired in Islamic conservatism (Malaysia is a Muslim-majority nation-state), that to most, still translates as the primacy of the collective over the individual, men over women, heteronormative over non-heteronormative, citizens over the stranger. These are not homogenous or monolithic categories (e.g. sexual citizens are treated as second-class citizens) as there are multiple axes of oppression at work. The capabilities, vulnerabilities and needs of women and those marginalised, even in the best of times, remain subordinate to the interests of those in dominant and powerful positions. Extolling the virtues of serving and submission as manifestations of hospitality *par excellence* fuels the social injustices already suffered, with structural violence intact (as some serve and submit more than others), and little reprieve for those most affected, in sight.

How do we encounter the stranger? Is hospitality, read as the protection of strangers and by extension, the least, the last and the lost, a moral responsibility that is only or best effected by spiritual grace (e.g. Biblical emphasis on neighbourliness) or legal obligations (e.g. 1951 Refugee Convention)? How are basic kindness and common decency (that turns out to be not so common) experienced and practised? Ilsup Ahn proposes yet another 'radical hospitality' that is predicated on a paradigm shift of hospitality from 'gift' to 'forgiveness'. Ahn problematises Derrida's 'absolute hospitality' that not only reinstates the mutually exclusive categories of giver and recipient (haves/haves-not) but also elides the 'invisible debt' that accompanies the 'idealization of hospitality as a form of gift'.[9] Ahn theorises from Derrida's deconstruction of a pure gift, as soon as a gift is given, and received as such, it annuls itself as a gift; and within the 'economy of gift', it slides into a 'form of debt' that positions citizens as creditors and refugees as debtors. The 'demonic power' that reeks from the 'hostility of debts' (resentment in giving and receiving), manifests as maltreatment of recipients as we have seen from the vitriol directed at asylum-seekers, refugees and migrants for arriving, overstaying and burdening those made more weary by the pandemic.

Within a 'paradigm of forgiveness', as Ahn posits, 'radical hospitality is understood as the creditor's self-payment of the invisible debt of the debtor';[10] the creditors' forgiveness of their debtors in emulation of 'God's forgiveness of all debtors through God's self-sacrifice'.[11] What sits uncomfortably about such a revised 'radical hospitality' is that Ahn has moved from the impossible gift to an impossible forgiveness (bordering on martyrdom). As Hamington, in her articulation of a 'theory of feminist hospitality', rightly notes, the 'history of women's oppression makes forgiveness a particularly challenging aspect of hospitality'.[12] I maintain that I had received the gift of encountering these refugee female leaders, humbly and gratefully, as did they, receive the gift of encountering me. We did not as such, start off with the social-ontological relationship of creditor-debtor. I was taken into their confidence despite my being, in their estimation, not like them. I was fed. I was sheltered. I was embraced. They were, under the auspices of the UNHCR, hospitable hosts in welcoming me, a stranger in their midst (they were familiar with each other as community leaders, often coming together for training). Our differences – age, nationality, class, education, ethnicity, religious persuasion, sexuality, gender identity and expression – before and after the encounters (including the mixed session with refugee male leaders), remained and shape who we have become but we are not reducible to these identity markers.

In sum, a theology of hospitality from a feminist-postcolonial lens is one of difference, mutuality and reciprocity. Respecting even proliferating differences as the *sine qua non* of diversity is akin to queering (making strange) hospitality as it avoids the tyranny of sameness (people like us who can return the gift), or as Letty Russell on practicing hospitality in a time of (feminist) backlash, posits, the 'pretence of unity through uniformity'.[13] The refugee female leaders and I were cognisant of our differentiated capabilities, vulnerabilities and needs that served to enrich our conversations and articulations of individual and collective aspirations of the past, present and future. Upholding mutuality in a divided world, resonates with Iris Marion Young's 'social connection model' that in holding each other accountable in redressing structural and systemic injustices, eschews a 'liability model' that deploys an infantile and harmful blame-game that detracts our urgent attention from the root causes of social injustices.[14] Through our inexhaustible narratives of childhood through to womanhood and motherhood for some, we shared an intense, reciprocal desire to optimise the brief time and space, preciously set aside for this transformative event; the encounter and exchange of ourselves. A radical ethics of hospitality starts with a care ethics of reciprocity that goes beyond acts of kindness in interrogating privileges and power as we inhabit our 'common home' differently – where many do not own a home.

Pope Francis in his encyclical, *Laudato Si'* exhorts us to ensure that "the quality of life of the poorest, are cared for…[as] we live in a common home which God has entrusted to us".[15] A radical hospitality from a feminist-postcolonial theological lens professes the profound relationality of the human, non-human (animals, ecology) and other-human (e.g. Artificial Intelligence). What's radical in that? Its absurdity, strangeness even queerness lies in recognising the stranger in ourselves and not misrecognising Christ Jesus in those not like us.

Notes

1. UNHCR-Malaysia, 'UNHCR-GoM Joint Action to Prevent, Manage Covid-19 Infections among Refugees'. *UNHCR-Malaysia-News*, 13 April 2020 at: https://www.unhcr.org/en-my/news/stories/2020/4/5e94189d4/unhcr-gom-joint-action-to-prevent-manage-covid-19-infections-among-refugees.html.
2. Emily Fishbein, 'Fear and Uncertainty for Refugees in Malaysia as Xenophobia Escalates', *The New Humanitarian*, 25 May 2020 at: https://www.thenewhumanitarian.org/news/2020/05/25/Malaysia-coronavirus-refugees-asylum-seekers-xenophobia.
3. Aihwa Ong, 'Translating Gender Justice in Southeast Asia: Situated Ethics, NGOs, and Bio- Welfare', *Journal of Women of the Middle East and the Islamic World*, 9, 1–2 (2011), 41.
4. Vinodoh Pillai, 'Blaming LGBT People For Covid-19 is Spreading Fast', *Queer Lapis*, 5 April 2020 at: https://www.queerlapis.com/blaming-lgbt-people-for-covid19/.
5. UNHCR, *UNHCR Policy on Age, Gender and Diversity*, March 2018 at: https://www.

unhcr.org/5aa13c0c7.pdf.

6. UNHCR Malaysia, 'UNHCR Representation In Malaysia', *UNHCR Malaysia* at: https://www.unhcr.org/en-my/unhcr-in-malaysia.html.

7. Jacques Derrida, *Acts of Religion*, New York and London: Routledge, 2002, pp. 360–361.

8. Maila Stivens, 'Family Values' and Islamic Revival: Gender, Rights and State Moral Projects in Malaysia', *Women's Studies International Forum*, 29 nr. 4 (2006), 356.

9. Ilsup Ahn, 'Economy of "Invisible Debt" and Ethics of "Radical Hospitality": Toward a Paradigm Change of Hospitality from "Gift" To "Forgiveness"', *The Journal of Religious Ethics*, 38, nr. 2 (June, 2010), 253.

10. Ibid., 258.

11. Ibid., 263.

12. Maurice Hamington, Toward a Theory of Feminist Hospitality, *Feminist Formations*, 22, nr. 1 (2010), 36.

13. Letty M. Russell, 'Practicing Hospitality in a Time of Backlash', *Theology Today*, 52, nr. 4 (1996), 478.

14. Iris M. Young, *Responsibility for Justice*, New York and Oxford: Oxford University Press, 2011 [online book].

15. Pope Francis, *'Laudato Si': On care for our common home'*, Vatican Press, 24 May 2015, paragraph 232 at: http://www.vatican.va/content/francesco/en/encyclicals/documents/papa-francesco_20150524_enciclica-laudato-si.html

Crossing Frontiers, Creating Other Possible Worlds: For a Decolonial Theology of Migration

CARLOS MENDOZA-ÁLVAREZ

This article sets out the initial coordinates for a decolonial theology of migration that draws on the experience, narratives and world view derived from the experience of individuals and peoples who migrate in search of a full life when, in the context of global violence, they suffer forced displacements. This gives rise to an 'ecclesiology of the communal' as an expression of cognitive and spiritual resistance on the part of migrant individuals and peoples who, through their fight for life, are members of the Messiah's queer body and a sign of kairological and anti-system anticipation of redemption.

I A Global Clamour: Migration as Forced Movement

Peoples have always migrated in search of life. Physical archaeology traces the empirical evidence of this human mobility, from the time of the hominids to the rise of *homo sapiens*. In this modern scientific narrative we can appreciate that the causes of migration have been diverse since the glaciations and the wars for fire and subsistence down to the famines and the imperial conquests that devastated peoples through their domination.[1]

From that remote past of humanity we know little about the subjective motivations of migration, the loves and hates, the obsessions and the phobias, the dreams and nightmares that persuaded people to leave their native soil or their community of origin. But we do know from the literature of the travellers who were seduced into crossing mountains, deserts and

30

seas to go looking for commodities, often motivated by intellectual or religious curiosity, seduced by the magnificence of the landscapes or kingdoms described in the reports of other travellers.[2] The Latin American literature of recent decades tells of the journeys into exile, many made for political reasons, that were the fate of social activists, intellectuals and artists fleeing military dictatorships.[3]

But Western modernity, while it was fed by these diverse motives of migration, deployed mechanisms of forced mobility to promote its economic and political power over the peoples of the globe, beginning with the trade in African slaves from the 16th century, which changed the face of cultures until it produced the transportations to concentration camps and refugee camps in the 20th century that are such a terrible memory.[4] Indeed, the North Atlantic wars of a few decades ago, together with totalitarian regimes in the rest of the planet, made more sophisticated the apparatus for controlling specific populations, allowing forced migrations for economic, racist, ideological and religious motives.[5]

At the beginning of the new millennium the globalisation of extractivist capitalism marked a qualitative change in migration, made more acute today by two unprecedented factors, climate change and the reduction to 'refuse' of the lives of whole peoples who are of no use to the global economy. As a result, forced mobility in these times of global war is reaching alarming levels, both for its reach over the population of the human race and for the dehumanisation it means for millions of people turned into subject masses crossing political, territorial and cultural frontiers. This floating population is seen as a threat by neocolonial peoples and governments, but can be dimly seen as a sign of incipient world change; this is the analysis from the perspective of the victims of the system themselves and of the transnational social movements that accompany them and create support networks for migrant and refugee people who are at high risk of pauperisation, falling into the power of criminal mafias and annihilation.

In this scene of social devastation on a planetary scale caused by forced migrations - in latitudes that go from the Mediterranean basin and the borders of the Sahara, to the route of the Beast (or the 'death train') in Mexico,[6] along which people from all over the globe travel under the watchful eye of the criminal mafias. These are just three emblematic routes of forced mobility in the global village. In the face of all this,

Christian theology is called to narrate, understand and make visible God's visitation of this fragmented history of humanity, the place where people live, paradoxically but in reality, an experience of divine-human grace as a kairos that anticipates the redemption.

II Decolonising frontiers through acts of resistance by migrant peoples

In the face of the necolonial expansion of capitalism based on 'enrichment by plunder and the extractive society',[7] promoted by governments of right and left to secure economic growth and social stability, acts of resistance by groups of people subjected to forced mobility grew in strength despite the suffering and injustice they were suffering. We must not forget that these individuals and populations really suffered from the acts of violence that went with their journeys: hunger, the extortion of the people-trafficking gangs, the rape of women, girls and LGBTIQ+ people, the racism and xenophobia of the communities they came into contact with on their way, the lack of spiritual support, and so many other forms of violence. On the other hand, we also need to emphasise the creativity with which these same individuals and groups, with the support of civil society and the churches, treated this experience of being uprooted as an opportunity to reinvent themselves in their poverty through various acts of resistance: they created networks of solidarity and support among themselves, refuges offering humanitarian assistance, centres for medical and legal advice and spaces for inter-religious spirituality promoted by civil society.[8]

The setting up of networks of refuges for migrant and refugee people is indeed a bright light amid the long night of exile. So too is the organising work done by the families, who, from the countries of origin or the destinations, accompany the uncertain route, condemn the people-traffickers' extortions and press governments – on all sides of the borders - to introduce migration policies that protect the lives and promote respect for the rights of people migrating or refugees. We know only too well that this is no more than a drop of solidarity in an ocean of avarice, corruption and injustice, but it is a powerful force to sustain the journey across different territories and frontiers, both physical and symbolic, in the hope that 'other worlds are possible' because they are desired, imagined and created out of this extreme vulnerability of having left the land, family and culture in which they were born and brought up as people and setting out towards the horizon of a new life.

Acts of resistance now become intertwined along the uncertain routes followed by the migrant peoples, whether among themselves or along with those who welcome them as neighbours protected by humanitarian or religious causes. This gradually creates the *ethos* or appropriate dwelling of a nomad people, which 'sets up its tent of meeting' in the midst of the inhospitable environment. The powerful metaphor of the Hebrew people from its constant exodus, diaspora and migration has been adopted in our time by the theology of migration.[9]

Rather than a romantic view of these experiences of mutual care between migrant and refugee people, I believe that the important aspect to stress here is the cognitive and spiritual force that develops out of the indignation, vulnerability and recognition that these people themselves experience. And moral indignation is certainly also political and spiritual because it is a cry that rises from the depth of the night, in the midst of an experience of forced exile that produces a cry for justice and life. Just here, in the midst of uncertainty, they discover the radical vulnerability of life, of the link with one's mother culture, of the ambiguous relationship with the other person who is a travelling companion but who may also be a threat. And nevertheless the mutual recognition of the people living this forced exile shines like a bright light when they protect each other on the road, when they tend the injured and the shipwrecked, when they bury their dead and when they carry on in spite of everything, and also thanks to the hands that offered them food and water and a space to rest with *apapachos*, caresses for body and spirit.[10]

The result is that the social movements' political awareness is matched by civil society and the churches when they establish 'sanctuaries' in the transit and destination countries in which a light of recovered humanity is consolation and balm of the wounded body of the human race.[11] This experience of acts of resistance produced from the extreme vulnerability endured by migrant and refugee people is a stronghold of wisdom for the whole of humanity. We shall explore this idea in the next section.

III Interculturality as a cognitive key

What are we to make of this phenomenon of forced mobility in the era of the global village in terms that go beyond the data and the systemic causes that give rise to it? We need to develop categories of critical thought that enable us to understand such personal and cultural traumas as the possibility of finding meaning in human nature, but in terms of the acts of cognitive resistance of the peoples who suffer it,[12] and no longer from the point of view of the killers who continue to impose their narratives as another form of domination and extermination.

Dismantling the neocolonial narratives and practices of the power of the system has a cognitive aspect. This implies insisting that the *wisdom* of people who migrate or are refugees is a moral and political stronghold, but also a cognitive and spiritual one that will allow us to go to the heart of the question of human nature in its dimensions of dignity in surviving and constructing inter-subjectivity in extreme conditions. In this way, overturning the supremacy of the narratives of the neocolonial trading posts that manipulate the arrival of crowds of migrants is what will make it possible to recover the knowledge of these second-class peoples forced to migrate when that knowledge has been rendered invisible.

This is why categories such as such as interculturality – invented by social anthropology and later reformulated as a dialogue of forms of knowledge by the epistemologies of the South and intercultural philosophy – are relevant to the task of outlining the shape of critical thinking that will contribute to raising the profile of the forms of knowledge of migrant peoples such as knowledge about care for life, social organisation and celebration of the harmony of the cosmos in intimate connection with the divinity. An example of this interchange of forms of knowledge is the 'mixed race theology' advocated by the Hispanic community in the United States, precisely as a theology of the 'mixing' that takes place when you cross borders and discover the humanity of the other as a moral and political call to do beyond an identity that dominates, subjugates and enslaves.

Another component of the interculturality advocated by recent Latin American philosophy is a critique of the 'objectifying' modernity that has made the world an object of measurement and power to underpin the privilege of the minorities that control the economies, politics and culture of peoples. An intercultural philosophy, according to the analyses of Raúl Fornet-Betancourt,[13] is one that relativises the West's ideas of universality and places them in relation to other forms of wisdom and rationality so that, among other components, they blend harmonically with the spiritualities of the peoples as genuine knowledge about humanity, the cosmos and the transcendent.

For all these reasons, interculturality as a cognitive key is a radical critique of the cultural model of domination imposed by the West in its commercial, religious and ideological expansion from the time of the voyages of conquest towards the end of the 15th century that exported Western rationality to all the latitudes of the planet. This expansion developed new forms of colonialism when the newly independent republics were incorporated into the dominant model of civilisation while their subject peoples were stripped of their resources.

But what has to be done now, in an age of globalisation and exclusion, is to use decolonial thought to undermine these foundations of colonisation, control of capital and patriarchy, which supported the tower of colonial power displaying the arms of white Christian religion. This complex system subjected the peoples to various forms of epistemicide that we now have to overthrow.[14]

IV The theological paradigm of the incarnation as a human-divine migration

The decolonial Christian theology that arises from listening to the cry of today's victims of the system is a second-level narrative that tries to understand the *redemption* that is possible in the midst of humanity's broken history through the survivors of all the violence.[15] In particular, for this theology of migration I am sketching out here, the wounded bodies of the migrant and refugee people who suffer forced mobility are a *sacrament* of the dismembered body of the Messiah that awaits the consolation of the divine Ruah which will bring to fulfilment the resurrection as an eschatological gift for humanity.[16]

This is why there is an urgent need to explore a theology of migration with a decolonial approach that will allow individuals and Church communities – in that love of neighbour that is the supreme expression of the new life brought by Christ – to stand alongside those who are forced to leave their land, their families and their culture in their yearning for a more just and more human world, possible because built by all as members of that messianic body in gestation as it crosses the fractures of humanity's broken history. In posthumously published remarks Ivan Illich formulated a theological truth from which today we need to extract the decolonial meaning, namely that Christ introduced into history a radical new meaning consisting in living out universal love of neighbour.[17] This truth has been corrupted, first by the Church and later by Western modernity by the institutionalisation of love as service, as it was delegated, first to Church bodies and then to legal and government bodies subsequently, and this is what is the very heart of redemption, living together as the principle of divine-human incarnation and the only way to achieve a redeemed creation.

How are we to understand, from this perspective of the incarnation of love of neighbour, the decolonial theology of migration? Who, and by means of what relationships, are the protagonists of redemption in this history of a humanity wounded by the system's violence? What experiences of closeness between and with migrant and refugee people are a source of meaning that enables us to understand the passage of God, who plants his tent in the migrant camp by analogy with the incarnation of the divine logos in Mary of Nazareth?

I believe that a decolonial theology of migration has to focus on the reality of the lives of those who suffer from this scourge in our time when the system wages war, in order to see there the signs of *communality* as an as an expression of the sociology of redemption that is, at root, an 'ecclesiology of the communal' understood through the diasporic bodies in exile, which are, in turn, subjectivities redeemed by being put back together as part of the queer body of the Messiah.[18]

And there, in all its splendour, will spring up the truth of the incarnation of the divine Word in Jesus of Nazareth as a radical expression of the compassion of God's Ruah with the force it deploys in those people who make those who are physically close true neighbours, a 'kairological' act that anticipates the redemption out of our rubble as a suffering but hope-filled humanity.

In this way the decolonial theology of migration will stammer the redemption that takes place in the migrant individuals and groups who rise up against the powers that try to keep them down in an insurrection fired by an experience of anger-compassion, bodiliness and dignity recognised, which offers grounds for hope to the whole of humanity, mortally wounded but promised to resurrection.

Translated by Francis McDonagh

Notes

1. Cf Fernando Díez Martín, *El largo viaje. Arqueología de los orígenes humanos y las primeras migraciones* (Barcelona, 2005).
2. An example of the history of the literature of migration in travellers' narratives can be found in Fernando Carmona Fernández, *Libros de viaje y viajeros en la literatura y la historia* (Murcia, 2006).
3. See the result of recent research on migrant writing in this cultural region of the planet in: Efrén Ortiz Dominguez and Isabelle Tauzin-Castellanos (ed.), *Viajes, exilios y migraciones: representaciones en la literatura latinoamericana del siglo XXI* (Xalapa, 2018).
4. International organisations such as UNHCR and the International Office for Migration regularly analyse the phenomenon of forced migration as a growing phenomenon, distinguishing internal displacement, refugees and applications for asylum, which increased significantly between 2009 and 2018: 'According to UNHCR, the number of forcibly displaced people both within countries and across borders as a result of persecution, conflict, or generalized violence has grown by over 50 per cent in the last 10 years; there were 43.3 million forcibly displaced people in 2009, and the figure was 70.8 million by the end of 2018 (UNHCR, 2019). Today 1 out of every 108 people in the world is displaced (ibid.)': https://migrationdataportal.org/themes/forced-migration-or-displacement (Accessed 30/11/2020).
5. Cf. Giorgio Agamben, *What is an apparatus? and other essays*, Stanford, CA, 2019.
6. For the case of Mexico as a constant channel of forced mobility migration of people from all over the world towards the United States, see the annual reports of the Documentation Network of Organisations Defending Migrants (REDODEM), especially the last two: REDODEM, *Procesos migratorios en México. Nuevos rostros, mismas dinámicas* (Mexico City, 2019) and *Migraciones en México: fronteras, omisiones y transgresiones* (Mexico City, 2020): http://redodem.org/wp-content/uploads/2019/09/REDODEM-Informe-2018.pdf (Accessed 30/11/2020).
7. See Raúl Zibechi, *Descolonizar la rebeldía. (Des)colonialismo del pensamiento crítico y de las prácticas emancipatorias* (Málaga, 2015).
8. See the special issue of *Concilium* devoted to the decolonial theology arising out of this resistance: Thierry-Marie Courau and Carlos Mendoza-Álvarez (ed.) *Concilium* 2020/1: *Decolonial Theology: Violence, Resistance and Spiritualities* (February 2020).
9. See Cioachinno Campese, *Hacia una teología desde la realidad de las migraciones. Métodos y desafíos* (Guadalajara, 2017).
10. *Apapachos* comes from a Náhuatl word describing a hug that reaches both body and heart.

11. See Ángeles Escrivá, Anastasia Bermúdez, and Natalia y Moraes, (ed.). *Migracióny participación política. Estados, organizaciones y migrantes latinoamericanos en perspectiva local-transnacional* (Madrid, 2009).

12. See an article that explores the relationship between migration and acts of cognitive resistance in terms of decolonial theory: José Carlos Luque-Brazán, 'Para comprender las migraciones internacionales en América (1990-2011): apuntes epistémicos, teóricos y empíricos', *Ánfora*, vol. 18, no 31 (July-December 2011), 141-163: https://www.redalyc.org/pdf/3578/357834264007.pdf (Accessed: 08/12/2020).

13. Since it was first proposed in 1994 until now, the idea of interculturality has been acquiring an increasingly precise philosophical sense, and now includes the forms of knowledge and spirituality of subjugated peoples who are recovering their epistemologies. See Raúl Fornet-Betancourt, *Hacia una filosofía intercultural latinoamericana* (San José, Costa Rica, 1994); 'Filosofía y espiritualidad en diálogo', *Concordia – Internationale Zeitschrift für Philosophie* 69 (2016).

14. The epistemic or cognitive wars in relation to the Maya have been analysed to reveal the forms of cognitive resistance adopted in the Zapatista autonomous regions and other processes of an ecology of knowledge. See Xóchitl Leyva, 'Pueblos en resistencia, justicia epistémica y guerra', *Cuadernos de Antropología Social*, No 14 (2016), 37-50: https://www.redalyc.org/pdf/1809/180951093003.pdf (Accessed 07/12/2020).

15. I have set out the case for a decolonial theology derived from the survivors in Carlos Mendoza-Álvarez, *La resurrección como anticipación mesiánica. Duelo, memoria y esperanza desde los sobrevivientes* (Mexico City, 2020). Brazilian edition: *A resurreição como antecipação messiânica*, São Paulo, 2020.

16. Here I am drawing on the queer theologies that are being developed in various cognitive contexts taken on by bodies from the diaspora in the transversality of acts of violence. See Stephanie Knauss and Carlos Mendoza-Álvarez (ed.), *Queer Theologies. Becoming the Queer Body of Christ*, *Concilium* 2019/5.

17. In a magisterial retrospective of his work, Illich said: 'My intention was to be able to talk to a contemporary audience about two things. The first is this mysterious and unprecedented glory, the thick phenomenological density that the body acquires under the influence of Christianity, under the influence of the Gospel, under the influence of the belief that a person who knocks at my door asking for hospitality will be treated by me as Christ, not as though they were Christ, but as Christ. And the second is how the secularisation of this faith produces that strange contemporary disincarnation, which is one of the most frightening experiences for people who have lived with their eyes open for the last twenty years' (Iván Illich, *Los ríos al norte del futuro. Conversaciones con David Cayley* (Mexico City, 2020, pp 147-148). English ed. *The Rivers North of the Future. The Testament of Ivan Illich as told to David Cayley*, Toronto, 2005. Translated from the author's Spanish.

18. This ecclesiology still has to be developed, in terms of the 'decolonial switch' produced by the epistemologies of the South and anti-system thought. See Juan José Tamayo-Acosta, *Teologías del Sur. El giro descolonizador* (Madrid, 2017). Key ideas from this perspective can be seen in José de Jesus Legorreta Zepeda, 'Diverse Communities Inhabited by the Divine Ruah', *Concilium* 2020/1, pp80-88.

Inforg:
A Boundary Between
Nature and Technology?

GIOVANNI GIORGIO

*Going beyond the debate raised by the cyborg theme, the author examines
the philosophical position of Luciano Floridi, who believes that ICT
(Information and Communication Technologies) does not consist merely
in applications which improve. Rather, the current computational ubiquity
is generating a new environment, the 'infosphere', which entails a new
ontology and a new macroethics. The first is based on the concept of
'informational object', and the second on an ontocentric vision that
includes every entity, natural or artificial. The outcome is a 'holistic
environmentalism' that promises a fruitful and symbiotic relationship
between technique and nature.*

The study I am offering here continues the research of one of my recent
publications,[1] in which, starting from *cyborg* understood as a *'cultural icon'*[2]
of our times, I set out to identify two fundamental tendencies competing
in this field: that of transhumanism, which opts for a 'separative' vision
between nature and technology, and the more properly posthumanist,
which opts for a 'hybrid' vision, in which the boundary between the two
appears intensely porous. It is precisely this latter point I wish to examine
in some depth here, going beyond what the reference to the cultural icon
of *cyborg*, a term around which there is on-going debate, has allowed me
to do to date. It is about the Luciano Floridi's philosophical suggestion,
which is particularly innovative, in his proposal of 'a marriage between
physis and *techné'*.[3]

I An analytical re-reading of the path of technology

To open the way for me, I am re-reading, with Luciano Floridi, about the path of technology, according to the analytical (not historical-chronological) progression he suggests.

The *first* step is represented by 'first-order technologies'.[4] These are focussed on the tool, that interface between humanity and the environment. Living non-humans are also capable of such technologies. The anthropological example could be provided by an axe for cutting wood. Floridi's summary schema is as follows:

humanity ← *technology* → nature

At least for the human threshold, interaction with the environment through an instrument produces in this case not just a modification of the environment, but also a retroaction on the person. In fact, if the environment is clearly vulnerable to technology, the human person also becomes vulnerable, in so far as technology disposes the human person to allow him- or herself to be shaped by it within a development system.[5] So if a development system which integrates nature (including human beings) and technology wants to keep itself alive at the evolutionary level reached, it will not be able to do so without the acquired technology, both in natural and artificial terms.

The *second* stage is represented by 'second-order technologies', focussed on the machine. The engine, understood as any technology which provides energy to other technologies, is probably the most important second-order technology. So, for example, roads do not require cars in order to be useful, but screws require a screwdriver. Floridi's schema is as follows:

humanity ← *technology* → technology

Floridi observes that 'much of late modernity – prompted by science's increasing knowledge about, and control over, materials and energy – gets its mechanical aftertaste from the preponderance of second-order technologies',[6] giving rise to 'a world of complex networked dependencies, of mechanical chain-reactions as well as locked-in connections: no trains

40

without railways and coal, no car without petrol stations and oil, and so forth, in a mutually reinforcing cycle that is both robust and constraining.'[7] In this case, too, more profoundly, the development system within which human beings live is vulnerable to technology, since increasingly the *seamless web* between natural (coal, oil, iron, etc) and artificial (trains, cars, etc) comes to condition the life of the system.

The *third* step is represented by 'third-order technologies'. In this case the technologies dialogue between themselves and take the place of humanity, making humanity's presence superfluous. Already we see its anticipations at work, for example, in the surveillance cameras everywhere, in the eyes of satellites, in vehicle-monitoring systems, in the 5G in smart cities, and in home automation. This implies that the 'threshold between *here* (analogue, carbon-based, offline) and *there* (digital, silicon-based, online) is fast becoming blurred, although this is as much to the advantage of the *there* as it is to the *here*. The digital-online world is spilling over into the analogue-offline world and merging with it. This recent phenomenon is variously known as '*Ubiquitous Computing*', '*Ambient Intelligence*', '*The Internet of Things*', or '*Web-augmented Things*".[8] Such a mechanism of artificial intelligence[9] is gradually being assembled around us, and is based on ICT. No-one knows its true magnitude, present or future. At this stage, ICT 'can process data autonomously and in smart ways, and so be in charge of their own behaviours. Once this feature is fully exploited, the human user may become redundant.'[10] The schema is the following:

$$technology \leftarrow technology \rightarrow technology$$

Now, a 'hyperhistorical society,'[11] fully dependent on third-order technologies can in principle be human-independent',[12] to the point of converging in an order in which human life, and nature more generally are located and from which they can be interpreted. In Floridi's words:

> computer science and the related ICTs have exercised both an extrovert and introvert influence on our understanding. They have provided unprecedented scientific insights into natural and artificial realities; but, in so doing, have cast new light on who we are, how we are related to the world and to each other, and hence how we conceive ourselves. At

41

present, we are slowly accepting the idea that we are not stand-alone, and unique agents, but rather are informational organisms (*inforgs*), mutually connected and embedded in an informational environment (the *infosphere*), which we share with other informational agents, both natural and artificial, that also process information logically and autonomously. Turing changed our philosophical anthropology as much as Descartes, Darwin or Freud.[13]

II A new anthology and a new ethics

It cannot be denied that ICT plays a decisive role in today's world, a role certainly played out at the level of global politics, where, by virtue of the phenomena linked to globalisation, we are witnessing what Floridi calls, using a biological analogy, political apoptosis, in other words 'the gradual and natural processes of renovation of sovereign states as they develop into information societies'.[14] What is important is the acknowledgement that ICT does not consist simply in 'applications which *improve* and applications which *increase*'[15] human performance or not. This distinction lies at the basis of the *cyborg* idea, but still lags behind compared to what is actually happening. ICT is an innovative reconfiguration of the reality in which are immersed. To speak with a certain fairness about the impact of this reconfiguration of the world,

we can use the neologism *re-ontologize* to refer to the fact that such a form [produced by the use of ICT] is not only limited to configuring, constructing or structuring a system (like a society, a car or an artifact) in a new way, but fundamentally involves the transformation of its intrinsic nature, that is to say of its ontology. In that sense, the ICTs are not only reconstructing our world, they are *re-ontologizing*.[16]

[ICTs] make us think about the world informationally and make the world we experience informational. The result of these two tendencies is that ICTs are leading our culture to conceptualize the whole reality and our lives within it in ICT-friendly terms, that is, informationally [...]. ICTs are modifying the very nature of, and hence what we mean by, reality, transforming it into an *infosphere*.[17]

The term 'infosphere' is a neologism coined by Floridi himself analogous to 'biosphere'. Just as in the biosphere various organisms find themselves to be interconnected, so it can be said that 'in many respects we are not isolated entities but rather inter-connected informational organisms (*inforgs*), which share with biological agents and engineered artifacts an informational environment (the *infosphere*).'[18]

This vision develops a true and proper ontology which, as has been noted, includes everything in a global system which Floridi identifies precisely as the infosphere. If, in fact, we take our discourse to a sufficiently high level of abstraction,19 in other words the level of being *qua tale*, every living being can be considered as an 'informational object'.[20]

> [T]hat means that [the information objects] are considered and treated as discrete, self-contained, encapsulated packages containing (i) the appropriate data structures, which constitute the nature of the entity in question: state of the object, its unique identity, and attributes; and (ii) a collection of operations, functions, or procedures (*methods*), which are activated (*invoked*) by various interactions or stimuli, namely messages received from other objects or changes within itself, and correspondingly define how the object behaves or reacts to them.[21]

In that sense, according to Floridi, it is fundamental to revise our conception of information,[22] considering it not just from the epistemological perspective as 'news', but also from the ontological perspective, as 'being'.

Such a position is functional to a final, decisive aspect of Floridi's position: the ethics he derives from these ontological premises, an ethic of information, which must not be confused with a local (or micro) information ethic, here only hinted at.

In effect, the ethics which Floridi suggests on these renewed bases, deriving from the 'ontological revolution'[23] in progress, can be proposed as maximally inclusive, since they espouse a perspective which is no longer anthropocentric, nor biocentric, although ontocentric, where ontocentric means focussed on what a being is, in other words an informational object.

What, then, is the most general possible common set of attributes which characterises something as intrinsically valuable and an object of respect, and without which something would rightly be considered intrinsically worthless (not just instrumentally useless or emotionally insignificant) or even positively unworthy and therefore rightly to be disrespected in itself? The least biased and most fundamental solution is to identify the minimal condition of possibility of an entity's least intrinsic worth with its nature as an information object. [...] Alternatively, to put it more concisely, being an information object qua information object is the minimal condition of possibility of moral worth and hence of normative respect. This is the central axiological thesis of any future Information Ethics that will emerge as a Macroethics.[24]

Such an information ethic assumes a broad spectrum minimal axiology, allowed by the underlying ontological premises, and 'suggests the idea that there is even something more elementary in life, that is being, that to say the existence and flowering of all beings and their global environment, and something even more fundamental than suffering, that is entropy.'[25]

As can be seen, the questions raised by Floridi's philosophical stance bring to our attention – with undeniable originality, but also with undeniable question marks – issues that the limitations of the article do not allow me to discuss.

III A holistic environmentalism

Given the premises set out up to this point, it will not be difficult to conclude that

The infosphere will not be a virtual environment supported by a genuinely 'material' world. Rather, it will be the world itself that will be increasingly understood informationally as an expression of the infosphere. [...] the infosphere will have moved from being a way to refer to the space of information to being synonymous with *reality* itself. This is the type of informational metaphysics we will find increasingly easy to make our own.[26]

This latter phrase seems all the more true the more we realise we are living immersed in a hyper-connected environment, the infosphere, in fact, which *per se* points towards what Floridi calls a 'holistic environmentalism';[27] in other words an environmentalism which does not favour the natural, but considers as authentic and original all forms of existence and behaviour, including those based on artificial, synthetic, or constructed artifacts. The direction which environmentalism opens is that of a 'marriage between *physis* and *techné*',[28] where nature 'and' technology, at this stage understood as the 'life environment' equal to nature, become one world in which everything is immersed.[29] However there remains the fact that a happy marriage, or as he says elsewhere, 'a virtuous circle between nature and technology'[30] is of vital importance for our future. If, in fact, we try to picture the world not of tomorrow or next year, but in a century or a millennium, the divorce between *physis* and *techné* would be totally disastrous both for our welfare and for the well being of our habitat. '[T]his is something that technophiles and green fundamentalists must come to understand. Failing to negotiate a fruitful, symbiotic relationship between technology and nature is not an option.'[31]

Translated by Patricia and Liam Kelly

Notes

1. Giovanni Giorgio, *Cyborg: il volto dell'uomo futuro. Il postumano fra natura e cultura*, Assisi: Cittadella, 2017. I can but refer to a future publication of mine in which I will investigate the relationship between nature and technology in various historical figures: the Greeks, medieval Franciscanism, the 'modern Synthesis' and, finally, the curent era, which I partly anticipate here. The provisional title is *Natura & tecnica. Sondaggi tra passato e presente*.
2. N. Katherine Hayles, *How We Became Posthuman. Virtual Bodies in Cybernetics, Literature, and Informatics*, Chicago & London: University of Chicago Press, 1999, 2.
3. Luciano Floridi, *Information. A Very Short Introduction*, Oxford: Oxford University Press, 2010. This work precedes the tetralogy which our author devotes to the fundamentals of the philosopjhy of information: *The Philosophy of Information*, Oxford: Oxford University Press, 2011; *The Ethics of Information*, Oxford: Oxford University Press, 2013; *The Logic of Information*, Oxford: Oxford University Press, 2019; *The Politics of Information*, in preparation. For this article I will refer exclusively to texts available in Italian.
4. Luciano Floridi, *The Fourth Revolution: How the infosphere is reshaping human reality*, Oxford: Oxford University Press, 2014, ch. II.
5. To clarify what I mean here by "development system" I refer to Susan Oyama, *The Ontogeny of Information. Developmental Systems and Evolution*, Second Edition Revised and Expanded, Foreword by Richard C. Lewontin, Durham (NC): Duke University Press, 2000. For a broader vision within which the question is placed, allow me to refer to Giovanni Giorgio, *Uno sguardo alle antropologie filosofiche attuali*, in Paolo Gherri (ed.), *Matrimonio e Antropologia. Un orizzonte per il Processo canonico. Atti della XII Giornata*

canonistica interdisciplinare, Città del Vaticano: Lateran University Press, 2019, 45-129.

6. Floridi, *The Fourth Revolution*, 28.

7. Floridi, *The Fourth Revolution*, 28.

8. Floridi, *The Fourth Revolution*, 43.

9. Once more proposing Turing's well-known text as a foundation, Floridi is clear in maintaining that a machine equipped with artificial intelligence behaves *as if* it were as intelligent as human beings. 'To use a domestic example, a dishwasher does not clean the plates like me, but at the end of the process its clean plates are indistinguishable from mine, they might even be cleaner. The same is true for AI. The example reminds us that we are talking about engineering, for which the result is important, not about cognitive science, where the agent or its behaviour are important, not the result, even if they are minimally intelligent. AI is not about reproducing human intelligence or producing a superiror intelligence, but about succeeding in doing without it, achieving the same or even better results. [...] In short, it is precisely when we stop trying to reproduce human intelligence that we can have succeded in resolving an increasing number of problems with AI'. Luciano Floridi, *Il verde e il blu. Idee ingenue per migliorare la politica*, Milan: Raffaello Cortina, 2020, 35-36.

10. Floridi, *The Fourth Revolution*, 32.

11. Thus writes Floridi, 'today, their [ICTs] autonomous *processing* capacities have ushered in a new, hyperhistorical age', Floridi, *The Fourth Revolution*, 167.

12. Floridi, *The Fourth Revolution*, 32. In fact, in this environment, humanity seems to be reduced to a 'semantic engine'. Floridi reports (*The Fourth Revolution*, 143) that ICTs, impervious to semantics, 'are not becoming more intelligent while making us more stupid. Instead, the world is becoming an infosphere increasingly well adapted to ICTs limited capacities', adding (146), 'One of the consequences of enveloping the world to transform it into an ICT-friendly place is that humans may become inadvertently part of the mechanism. The point is simple: sometimes our ICTs need to *understand* and *interpret* what is happening, so they need semantic engines like us to do the job. The fairly recent trend is known as *human-based computation*.'

13. Luciano Floridi, *Pensare l'infosfera. La filosofia come design concettuale*, trans. Massimo Durante, Milano: Raffaello Cortina, 2020, 130.

14. Floridi, *The Fourth Revolution*, 169. For more detail on the political questions to which an information society gives rise at both state and global level, see the whole of ch 8, as well as all of Floridi, *Il verde e il blu*, especially the summary, ch. 19.

15. Floridi, *La rivoluzione dell'informazione*, 12.

16. Floridi, *La rivoluzione dell'informazione*, 13.

17. Floridi, *The Fourth Revolution*, 40. Elsewhere Floridi adds that 'in some cases one can already begin to speak about a mature information society, where life passes by now *onlife*, within a digital space [*online*] and analogical space [*offline*] which can be called *infosphere*'. Floridi, *Il verde e il blu*, 62.

18. Floridi, *La rivoluzione dell'informazione*, 11. The movement is from an Ur-philosophy focussed on things, to an Ur-philosophy focussed on relationships.

19. 'A level of abstraction qualifies the level at which a system is considered. [...] It is fundamental to observe that the assessment and corresponding preference for an LoA [level of abstraction] is dictated, as a rule, by the purpose driving the original request for information. [...] We can therefore agree that a system is characterised, at a given LoA, by the properties it satisfies at that level of LoA'. Floridi, *Pensare l'infosfera*, 59-60. This is like saying there are different levels of access to reality which are dependent on the starting

perspective, the perspective from which we observe and interpret things, which, starting from the questions possible at that level, respond to us in a satisfactory manner.

20. Floridi is keen to note that it would be wrong to believe that beings 'are necessarily

only informational objects'. (Luciano Floridi, *Infosfera. Etica e filosofia nell'età dell'informazione*, Introduction by Terrell Ward Bynum, trans. Massimo Durante, Torino: Giappichelli, 2009, 78.) In the example in the text Mary may be considered alive, as a mammal, as a gendered human being, a social being, an Anglo-Saxon citizen, and so on, according to the chosen level of abstraction. And nevertheless at a specific level of abstraction which, as far as I understand, coincides with being itself, Mary, like every other being, whether natural or artificial, can be considered informational object.

21. Floridi, *Infosfera*, 79.

22. For the concept of information, cf. Floridi, *La rivoluzione dell'informazione*, ch. 2.. For a broader discussion about the concept of information and its influence see, Paolo Vidali, Federico Neresini, *Il valore dell'incertezza. Filosofia e sociologia dell'informazione*, Milan-Udine: Mimesis, 2015; James Gleick, *The Information: A History, a Theory, a Flood*, Fourth Estate, 2011; Charles Seife, *Decoding the Universe: How the new science of information is explaining everything in the cosmos, from our brains to black holes*, Viking Books, 2006.

23. Floridi, *La rivoluzione dell'informazione*, 129.

24. Floridi, *Infosfera*, 95. Other macroethics examined by Floridi to reveal their limitations are deontologism, consequentialism and contractualism. Cf. Floridi, *Infosfera*, ch. 1. See also, *La rivoluzione dell'informazione*, ch. 8.

25. Floridi, *La rivoluzione dell'informazione*, 140.

26. Floridi, *La rivoluzione dell'informazione*, 21-22.

27. Floridi, *La rivoluzione dell'informazione*, 149.

28. Floridi, *La rivoluzione dell'informazione*, 149.

29. It seems to me that Luciano Floridi places himself in the wake of the phenomenological and/or post-phenomenological approach of the philosophy of technology, focussed on relationships between human beings and the technical environment, but going beyond it. For this approach cf. Don Ihde, *Technology and Lifeword: From Garden to Earth*, Bloomington IN/Indianapolis: Indiana University Press, 1990; Andrew Feenberg, *Between Reason and Experience: Essays in Technology and Modernity*, Boston: MIT Press, 2010; Robert Rosenberg and Peter-Paul Verbeek (eds.), *Postphenomenological Investigations: Essays on Human-Technology Relations*, London: Lexington Books, 2015.

30. Floridi, *Il verde e il blu*, 257.

31. Floridi, *La rivoluzione dell'informazione*, 150.

Theology as Border-Crossing:
Lessons from a Hostel for Refugees

STAN CHU ILO

This essay develops three steps for a theology of border-crossing that is capable of birthing a creative and transformative culture of encounter for embracing our shared identity as humans in the rising contestations about identity and exclusion in the Church and in the world. The essay shows how the Church can be a space for encountering the other through practices and priorities which make possible the crystallization of the inclusive love of God as the centre around which there are no borders and walls. The paper concludes by showing how theological border-crossing could be a form of theological perichoresis modelled after the Trinitarian perichoresis because it weaves multiple paths, traditions, histories, and identities as an art and spiritual exercise that invites individuals and communities of faith to a dynamic celebration of the dignity and beauty of differences. The possibility of a theology of border-crossing capable of translating the boundless love of God into pastoral and social praxis is shown also as a personal and communal pilgrimage for individuals, churches, nations, races and indeed all people beyond the claims of nativism and indigeneity.

One of my best experiences of living outside my home country, Nigeria, was the three months that I spent as a resident of a male hostel for refugees which was ran by *Centro di accoglienza internazionale-Ostello della Gioventù* of the Archdiocese of Perugia. I commuted from this hostel to the Italian language school at the *Università per Stranieri* di Perugia. The Archdiocese of Perugia gave me a temporary residency here which offered me a privilege of immersing myself into the painful stories of the refugees and illegal immigrants in Europe. My residential unit had six refugees (from Somalia, Djibouti, Palestine, Haiti, Cuba, and Sudan) all of whom had no papers (*permesso di soggiorno*) to stay in Italy. Each of them shared some painful stories of their perilous journeys, some across the Mediterranean; others across different borders of many countries, and others through a 'miraculous escape' from their countries, courtesy of one agency or another, or through some unscrupulous criminal networks who preyed on vulnerable people in Latin America, Africa, and the Middle East.

All of us in this hostel were, however, united by one reality: we were all strangers in a foreign land. Thus, we saw in each other something of our shared needs, our social dislocation and vulnerabilities, and sought in each other a social bond and love that made concrete to all of us our common humanity. Even though we were a diverse group (Catholics, Protestants and Muslims) from different parts of the world and from diverse cultural and linguistic backgrounds, there was an amazing closeness between us that felt for me like a little taste of heaven. This forced me to reimagine a space like this, not only in Europe, but in every part of the world where our ethnic, racial, gender and religious differences often lead to discrimination, intolerance, and exclusionary social hierarchies that harm our collective existence and poison shared spaces for human flourishing.

What I share in this essay is what the experience of living with these siblings of mine taught me about (1) our shared identity as humans vis-à-vis the contestations about identity today; (2) the Church as a space for encountering the other in an inclusive love of God who centres our being and history in a boundless love as the dynamism of all things; and (3) the possibility of a theology of border-crossing that translates the boundless love of God into pastoral and social praxis. Such a theology of border-crossing can only emerge when a theologian embraces his or her own vulnerability and that of others on these margins of human experience, dislocation and self-surrender.

I Beyond the Boundaries of Identity and Otherness

My community of refugees at this hostel offered me a sense of bondedness and friendship which was different from what I experienced outside this community. It became crystal clear to me in my first interactions with white people outside my migrant community that the acceptable colour-code was white and that being black is a marginal reflection in this colour-coded spectrum. I was, however, challenged to stretch my gaze beyond my own experience to pay greater attention to our common human hunger and what faith, the Church, and theology could offer in creating an understanding and practices of belonging so that they could fully experience the true sense of being persons within a community (*Fratelli Tutti*, 182). But this requires understanding the reasons for boundaries and an analysis of how power and *othering* function in creating boundaries. As Toni Morrison writes, "for humans as an advanced species, our tendency to separate and judge those not in our clan as the enemy, as the vulnerable and the deficient needing control, has a long history not limited to the animal world or prehistoric man. Race has been a constant arbiter of difference, as have wealth, class, and gender—each of which is about power and the necessity of control."[1]

Pope Francis writes in *Fratelli Tutti* that in the face of "present efforts to eliminate or ignore others", and in a world "bristling with watchtowers and defensive walls" as it was in the time of St. Francis, we need to build a world without borders. This is the world where we can dream of "a single human family, as fellow travellers sharing the same flesh, as children of the same earth which is our common home, each of us bringing the richness of his or her beliefs and convictions, each of us with his or her own voice, brothers and sisters all" (FT, 8). This is the ideal which a theology of border-crossing aims at realizing for people of faith. However, bringing to birth that world without walls—in both theological and metaphoric sense—does require understanding the reasons why people build walls and the diversity of worldviews. Fears, cultural projects, and religious narratives are often employed in the erection of these walls which serve as identity markers for so many people.[2]

The question of identity—the in-group vs. the out-group—is indeed a human conundrum which has been at the root of many of the horrible evils in human history—racism, genocide, Nazism, sexism, religious wars and persecution, nationalism and homophobia, anti-immigration sentiments, to mention only a few. Human identity in our contemporary times has become 'liquid' (Zygmunt Bauman), fluid, transitional, and contested. Pamela

Young and Heather Shipley in a recent ethnographic study of Canadian youth found that most of them see themselves primarily as authors of their own identities and that their sense of who they are is open to ongoing self-construction.[3] On the other hand, for most people today, their identities are often defined by social norms and the authorization of roles or denial of roles within some clearly defined unmovable boundaries. One needs only to look at the labels we assign to people based on identities. Some of these labels are created through social-constructionist paradigms. In this regard, one sees that "the stigmatization of an identity" emerges from social relationships, and traditions which create social hierarchies and practices and systems of marginalization. This is why Cathy Cohen underlines as a counterpoint the need to appreciate the malleability of identities which regularly must contest, and disrupt dominant norms in society.[4]

This line of argument has been taken up by the African philosopher, Anthony Appiah who argues against a rigid classification of peoples based on such categories like religion, sexuality, nationality, culture, class and race. In *Cosmopolitanism*, he draws attention to contesting universalities as essential to understanding the present global angst about fossilized notions of identity. He proposes that society must embrace a cosmopolitan spirit, acceptance, and toleration of the *other*.[5] In *Lies that Bind*, Appiah recognizes that identity gives people labels. Claims of identity most times can help us see clearly the sources and motivations for people's actions for or against other people outside their own identity group. However, he proposes that we should not absolutize identities. Rather, we should pay particular attention to how identities provide normative significance for systems and structures of power, exclusion vs. inclusion within a particular identity group or against people outside the identity group. This is why he proposes that while we may not dispense with identities all together, "we need to understand them better if we can hope to reconfigure them, and free ourselves from mistakes about them that are often a couple of years. Much of what is dangerous about them has to do with the ways identities divide us and set us against one another."[6]

The borders of belonging and exclusion which have been mapped by peoples, cultures, races, genders and classes are often false. Zygmunt Bauman asserts, for example, that boundary designs are often "the self-definitional and self-assertive interests of its carriers" in the contestation for economic or political power. Exclusive identity markers lead to boundaries being drawn not because of any threats to co-existence or systemic changes that could create a more equitable social life, but because of multiple layers of factors. These factors are often the result of many years of obfuscation of reality leading to false narratives of the *other*, stereotypes, 'incongruous mixture' of types and frames which define *the other* without the other's voice, and reinscribe vices or denies value to the *other* in ways that make the rejection of the *other* or his or her *non-recognition* possible.[7]

Our diverse human identities should not turn us into inmates incarcerated in narrow cultural, national, racial, ethnic, religious, and gender prisons. Rather, it should free us to love and to see each person as someone beautiful to God. The term, "child of God," is the identity that is the central foundation of theological anthropology—the human person is made in the image and likeness of God. The story of the Christian God in both testaments of the scripture can only lead us to one conviction "that persons are brothers and sisters in a single human family that reaches across borders."[8] An African theological anthropology affirms a relational bond among people in an expansive notion of community. African anthropological reasoning on community upholds a sacred bond with God, nature, and with one another as the condition for preserving and promoting the common good, that is, the abundant life of the community. In this light, it is only in participating in the joys and sorrows of others and sharing in the travails of creation that we realize our true identity. Thus, by increasing a shared bond of love, participation, and mutuality through acts of solidarity and self-surrender and by embracing an expansive notion of community beyond ourselves, we create the conditions for human and cosmic flourishing.

Ultimately, contestations about identity, exclusion, rejection, and stereotypes of people which have defined the global order and created social hierarchies in our world today can only be understood through an analysis and critique of power and privilege.[9] This analysis of power and interests will help to expose the deep insecurities, individualism, and narrow interests of a few; and the vulnerabilities and hidden wounds in our world today. The struggle in today's world, and the pathos of so many are only signs that people are struggling with the new challenges emerging from past histories of injustice, destructive global economic systems, cultural, religious and ecological practices which have created so much exclusion, poverty, racism, nativism, nationalism, anger, hatred and suffering in the world.

A more inclusive world and a more inclusive Church can begin first when people have the courage to go beyond our human, cultural, national, racial, and theological fortresses. We can reimagine new ways of seeing human diversity, and a compassionate look on those who are suffering at the various walls built by religious, economic, and political systems to exclude them. This reimagination could lead theologians and church leaders to ceaselessly search for new ways of rebuilding our social bonds, a new way in which the Church can mirror the kind of world that reflects the signs of the eschatological fruits of God's kingdom.

II The Church as a Field Hospital without borders

Another lesson I learned at the migrant hostel was that it offered me a different site for reimagining a different kind of church. Here, I experienced a different kind of direct encounter with Christ in the *other* which was real and concrete. I felt such moments during our common meals usually once a week. These meals offered me a rare moment in my own personal pilgrimage to experience a church without borders as I travelled beyond my own biases, fears, and securities to regions of transcendence where the *other* is present to me in radical affinity that conveys to me a real presence of the divine and a reflection of my true self.

We all took turns to prepare this weekly meal; each person is encouraged to cook a traditional meal from his own culture. While gathered around the table and joining hands in prayer, each took turns to say a prayer in his own religious tradition and in his own language. This was followed by a meal at which we shared our stories of what happened that week; anecdotes from our respective countries, and the joys and sorrows from the uncertain paths each of these siblings of mine walk every day in search of the needed immigration documents, work or money to meet their needs and that of their families at home. At this table, all our differences and fears melted away. Prayers were said by each for all. We learned some words from the other's languages and imbibed social norms from our respective cultures. We were all crossing and transgressing multiple borders and immersing ourselves in the narratives of each other which was very transformative for us all.

At the weekly meal, all housemates took turn to serve each other. No one had a special seat; everyone had a shared experience of receiving and giving love as a form of service and solidarity. It is notable as I reflected on this experience that the Catholic Archdiocese of Perugia made this encounter possible by opening its doors to the strangers. We were thus provided with a space where we could share our stories and be at home with one another. In this encounter, our individual identities did not dissolve into sameness, but were transformed into a presence to each other that transported us to regions of inclusiveness, where our differences no longer mattered to us because we became brothers to all. I was the only Catholic in the cohort, but there was a friendship that developed among us which relativized our differences and harmonized them into a form of celebration and solidarity.

The migrant hostel offered me what Peggy Levitt calls "a transnational gaze" which was liberating and also challenging. I began to see the possibility of holding in a healthy balance the tension between cosmopolitan universalism and nationalistic or ethnocentric or racial particularism. A transnational gaze "begins with a world that is borderless and boundaryless, and then explores what kinds of boundaries exist, and why they arise in specific times and places. It tries hard not to overemphasize the global or the local but to hold these social layers, along with everything in between, in productive conversation with each other...It recognizes that some social processes happen inside nations while many others, though rooted in nations, also cross their borders."[10] An ecclesial transnational gaze is properly a Catholic gaze because here we are invited to see the catholicity of our faith communities and our world through the lens of diversity that mirrors the Trinitarian origin of the Christian and ecclesial life. It invites one to reimagine what the Church would look like if we looked at people and the world as God looks at them beyond existing frames and stereotypes constructed through metanarratives that use a single story to encompass all the immense diversities of our human stories.[11]

The Church is a site for the re-telling of the Gospel story in the narratives of the joys and sorrows of God's people today. In the migrant hostel in Perugia, I read the text of the Gospel in a site created by a Catholic community. Sharing the stories of my hopes and despair with my housemates, and listening to the stories of my housemates and their fears, anxieties, distress, and dreams became my weekly encounter with God's word enacted in new ways. In these stories, I experienced how the face of the Church looks like when it offers a capacious tent like this hostel, where many who have crossed several borders in their search for survival can find a home in a borderless site where love and friendship meet. Here, I experienced the deepest bonds of love which *Gaudium et Spes* (GS 1) affirms as the Trinitarian origin of the Church and of the human family.

The church is not our giant cathedrals and resplendent buildings. It is the people of God in their sites of pain and panic in the face of Covid-19; it is the housemates in whose lives I shared for three months in Perugia. It is any site where we can give and receive love and thus make Christ present and real. The church is never a fixed structure; it is the dynamic movement of God's people called to travel especially in our times in the painful road of tears, silence, wounds, and pain in the hope of the Resurrection. This ecclesiological image challenges the church today to embrace a more creative search for the faces of Christ in the wounded faces of the world today. It should shatter the attachment to fixed boundaries, exclusionary practices, and stubborn attachment to traditions which have grown old and those cultic acts, and ranks which often can hold the church and her members enslaved to the past or to repetitive communal practices which dull the spiritual perceptivity in seeing the surprises of the Holy Spirit and the signs of the times in finding God in unseemly places.

The image of the church as a field hospital also reminds us of the pilgrim nature of our earthly life and the pilgrim character of the church which shatters the binding claims of nativism and indigeneity born of cultural hubris and superiority complex of any kind. Indeed, the word "parish" *(paroikos)* refers to a pilgrim, someone who is living temporarily in a place, an alien, someone residing in a foreign land. Covid-19 has made this meaning of a parishioner more real for everyone—the transitory nature of our lives, the field hospitals where faith is being put in action in our cities, food banks, and other places where love is being born anew in our world. But this transitory nature of life or rather the pilgrim nature of our shared life, and the richness of the capacious openness of the church to the *other* was a reality which came alive so clearly and concretely for me at the migrant hostel in Perugia.

III Theology as Border Crossing: A Sacred Dance with God

There are three lessons and practices which the refugee hostel taught me on how to do theology.

First, leaving my home country and taking up residency in the home for refugees. Theology as border-crossing begins with a movement of the heart—a dislocation. This movement is often initiated through an experience or an encounter with otherness in which the theologian loses his or her self-possession. It is a form of mystical experience as one is totally taken up not in the preservation of the self, but in the finding of the face of God in the other. It is thus a shift from the centre to the margins. This movement shatters our sense of safety, breaks the walls of indifference and boundaries of exclusion through a *Catholic gaze* that sees all things as God sees them beyond the limit of our human horizon.

This dislocation creates a form of insecurity because like an alien one is afraid of losing one's ground. However, what happens at the borders of human experience is that we are stepping on holy ground in the presence of the *other,* especially those who like any of us, are displaced and searching for a home. It is through this movement that a wider vista is opened for the theologian to see the ever-widening sites of God action in history beyond our comfort zones.

Theology as border-crossing is thus an invitation to do theology as a vulnerable and humble embrace of the stories of God as we receive them in reverential encounter with the stories of others, and in our own honest acceptance of the limits of our own securities, vulnerabilities, and settled conclusions about reality and the *other.* In making this movement, we step out of our own world and enter into a new world that is larger than our own experiences, cultural habitus, labels, frames, and egos. We enter into a new space that is capable of expanding our personal boundaries by enlarging our sense of community.[12]

Second, *finding a home in a shared space at the refugees' centre where none of us could claim any exclusivity, but rather a shared home defined by social friendship and mutual solidarity.* Theology of border-crossing shifts our way of thinking and epistemic frames. It is a movement from dislocation to a location. This is about becoming more aware that the locus of enunciation of the theologian are the sites where God is present beyond the road well-travelled. African theologian, Jean-Mac Ella, proposes that theology is "an itinerary of self-discovery on a road travelled with others, in the direction of Christ, toward whom all converges."[13] In this journey, the theologian must suspend judgement, and follow the stories of people. S/he becomes an actor in the drama of life with others and not simply as a spectator or a disinterested commentator. It is in travelling this road with the other that the theologian can learn a new language and gain new knowledge. The stories of the wounded on the road will become the location where theologians like the good Samaritans can contribute in healing those who have been battered by some of our exclusionary social, economic, cultural and ecclesial practices.

The theologian too bears his or her own wounds and tears. In speaking from and to these wounds with hope as theologians and pastors to the community, we are reimagining our communities of faith as vital churches and sites for healing and acceptance as well as maternities for delivering new lives in the birth pangs of creation. When we open our hearts to the grace of God, and when we accompany those whose hearts are searching for love, acceptance, and for healing, we find that our human heart becomes the location where our individual and communal fragilities become generative of life, love and hope. This transformation is aided by the irruption of God's boundless and unrestricted love, that always becomes operative through transformative grace when we encounter others as God would encounter them.

Third, beginning to reimagine a common future and recreating a new history from our shared stories and dreams at the home for refugees. Theological border-crossing is a craft of the heart, an intellectual art, and a spiritual exercise that leads to performance—it is a way of life for the theologian because it takes hold of the heart, the head, and the hand of the theologian. It is the conversion of the whole person in the face of a true encounter that leads to an identification with the other that is incarnational. This approach to doing theology is capable of transforming theology and the vocation of the theologian today so that he or she can go beyond the dualism and polarizations in the World Church and the wider society to discovering the face of God in the other.

This approach to doing theology can properly be termed theological perichoresis because it is an invitation to weave the intersecting paths of so many lives through attention to the rich tapestry of our beautiful and diverse human stories modelled by the sacred dance of the three persons in One God. Just as the three divine persons share a common life and friendship, receive and are indwelling in one another in a diversity of operation and unity of essence so also does a theological perichoresis function as a border-crossing that embraces the *other* with respect, solidarity, and recognition without suppressing or erasing otherness or differences. Just as the three divine persons by working together in a dynamism of love, bring about creation; so also, a theological perichoresis holds in a healthy balance diverse human identities, and cosmic realities, complex differences of opinions, beliefs, and practices in a way that a new history, a new creation and a new understanding is always emerging from these differences in our theological imagination and praxis.

This way of doing theology which re-presents these diverse stories as the footprints of God in history makes theology authentic, aesthetic, credible, concrete and hope-filled. Theology can then become a form of daily practice, a walking together with the *other* that transforms both the theologian and his or her faith communities into doers of God's will and builders of vital and resilient communities of faith. This movement from dislocation, to location, and from a location that is borderless to constructing a new history by accompanying *the other,* nourishes an ecclesial culture of encounter through a theological openness to the surprising new things made possible through the Holy Spirit in the continuing renewal of creation. It is both an art to be cultivated, and a form of worship. Indeed, it is only through transgressing the boundaries of *otherness* that we can truly encounter that centre of boundless love—Christ—who always shatters our boundaries when we encounter him truly in the sick, the forgotten, the abandoned, the stranger, the thirsty, and the rejected and in all human beings in their thirst for love and acceptance.

Notes

1. Toni Morrison, *The Origin of Others*. Cambridge: Harvard University Press, 2017, 3.

2. Joseph Carens and Philip Marfleet have argued that the time has come for borders to be made open for those who are facing humanitarian crisis. See David Hollenbach, *Humanity in Crisis: Ethical and Religious Response to Refugees*. Washington, DC: Georgetown University Press, 2019, 64.

3. Pamela Young and Heather Shipley, *Identities under Construction: Religion, Gender, and Sexuality among Youth in Canada*. Montreal: McGill University Press, 2020, 108.

4. Cathy Cohen, *The Boundaries of Blackness: AIDS and the Breakdown of Black Politics*. Chicago: The University of Chicago Press, 1999, 38-39.

5. Anthony Appiah, *Cosmopolitanism: Ethics in a World of Strangers*. NY: W. W. Norton and Company, 2006, 144.

6. Kwame Anthony Appiah, *The Lies that Bind: Rethinking Identity*. NY: Liveright Publishing Corporation, 2018, xvi.

7. Zygmunt Bauman, Modernity and the Holocaust. NY: Cornell University Press, 1989,41-43.

8 David Hollenbach, *Humanity in Crisis: Ethical and Religious Response to Refugees*, 72

9. On how identity politics functions in the world today see *Francis Fukuyama, Identity: The Demand for Dignity and the Politics of Resentment*. NY: Farrar, Straus, and Giroux, 2018, 115-118.

10. Peggy Levitt, *God Needs no Passport: Immigrants and the Changing American Religious Landscape*. London: The New Press, 2007, 22-23.

11. Richard Bauckham, *Bible and Mission: Christian Witness in a Postmodern World*. Grand Rapids: Baker Book, 2005, 4.

12. Palmer, Parker, The *Courage to Teach: Exploring the Inner Landscape of a Teacher's Life. S*an Francisco: Jessey-Bass, 1998, 120.

13. Jean Mac Ela, *Africa Cry*, trans. Robert R. Barr. Maryknoll, NY: Orbis Books, 1986, 23.

Part Two: The Case Study: Europe and the Mediterranean Sea

Borderline Europe:
On the Ambiguity and the Drivers of
the European Border Regime

MICHELLE BECKA AND JOHANNES ULRICH

In view of the humanitarian catastrophe on Europe's borders, this article seeks to outline the drivers and the ambiguity of European border regulation and make a suggestion on how to deal with the (European) crisis. After a short introductory reflection on the concept of borders and performative border practices in the sense of 'doing borders', it offers an analysis of the changes and the status quo in European border regulations in recent years. In this setting limits and exclusion stand out as important elements of the EU's border system. The conclusion looks for possibilities for solidarity along vertical borders, that is between the institutions, towns, regions and the EU as a whole.

This article is being written in the first weeks of the pandemic caused by the virus SARS-CoV-2. The events of these months have left our eyes glued to the topic, a virus that neither natural nor political borders seem to stop, a wide-ranging limitation of public life, accompanied by a reimposition of internal borders in the EU. On top of this there is the worsening of the humanitarian catastrophe on Europe's borders, where 42,000 refugees in the camps on Lesbos – as it were, both locked out and locked up – were living packed together.[1] 'Social distancing' on one side of the border, inadequate water supplies on the other.

But precisely because of the rapidly changing 'current situation', and looking beyond it, the first question we ask in this article is about the significance of borders in general, and stress their ambiguity. After the general considerations there is a close focus on the problems of European borders: how could it be that a continent without borders became – and not just because of corona – a 'fortress Europe'? Finally, horizontal and vertical borders are explored in search of spaces of action that can make possible new forms of solidarity.

I Fences and their functions

The prototype of the border is the fence. A fence separates what is mine from what is another's and points to the fact that the connection between territory and property is an etymologically old and important strand of meaning in the concept of the border. A fence is also a clear order *not* to cross this boundary. But 'a limit and a transgression are mutually dependent for their density: there is no such thing as a limit that it would be absolutely impossible to breach.'[2]

Boundaries, in other words, are in principle crossable. A fence usually has a hole or a gate – the boundary *can* be crossed. At the same time someone determines, or there is a negotiation about, who is and is not allowed to cross this boundary. Boundaries are constructed between these poles of ability and permissibility. They are barriers that prevent crossing. They are filters, since some people are allowed to cross. They discriminate, limit and exclude.

Discrimination means emphasising distinctions. This implies two characteristics that are either separated from each other or whose existing separation is reinforced. *Something* is always distinguished from *something else*. In the process the boundary is the imaginary line that often produces the distinctions in the first place. Once the boundary is drawn, separation gains the upper hand over commonality. The stress on distinction contrasts with the constructed nature and contingency of that imaginary line: the boundary is where it is – but couldn't it just as well be somewhere else?

Putting boundaries round what is mine has an effect on the other, what lies beyond the boundary. While the field of meaning of the concept of the boundary initially includes the areas on this side and on the other side of the boundary without distinction, what is over the boundary later increasingly disappears from the picture, and the boundary increasingly becomes the end-point of this side.[3] And behind that? *Hic sunt leones*, 'Here be lions,' as was noted on Roman and medieval maps beyond the boundaries of the then known world. Over there, in that view, whose influence lives on, is the alien, danger, what is unordered.

This idea of the boundary as an end-point reveals the connection between territory and recognition. While the process of making a distinction requires a knowledge of the other side, so that its order can be recognised as an order different and distinct from the order on this side, when attention is concentrated exclusively on this side, this knowledge loses significance. In the worst case it is even denied. Here we have order, there there is chaos. Consequently the idea of defence replaces thoughts that were concerned with negotiating the differences.

Erecting boundaries goes with exclusions: of people who are different, different ways of thinking, different ways of organising things, different ways of life, etc. On the other hand, it seems that practices of exclusion have long ago become detached from the concept of a boundary, at least in the case of a national frontier. Or, to put it in other terms, the dynamic of drawing boundaries becomes clear. The issue the is less about understanding what boundaries are than what having boundaries means,[4] how they are fixed and moved. But this shows that that the everyday social techniques of exclusion are after all not so far removed the concept of a boundary – including national frontiers. Having boundaries also applies to national frontiers. As (boundary) practices they are not static; they are set and depend on political processes that can be described as a frontier system.

Following these general considerations, we shall analyse the frontier system of the European Union. Alongside the abolition of frontiers and the opening up of areas for negotiations, this will prove to be a frontier system that practises inward limits and outward exclusion.

II The short step from Schengen to Dublin

For more than 25 years the internal European borders have no longer been frontiers for people. Barriers and frontier checks have faded from people's memories, and the new frontier-less world has become a fixture in the lives of Europeans: travel, pupil exchanges, study trips, cultural and sporting projects have over the years created a sense of not being just German, Spanish, French or Austrian, but also European.

'Anxious to strengthen the solidarity between their peoples by removing the obstacles to free movement at the common borders,'[5] said the parties of themselves as they signed up to this unique project in the Luxembourg town of Schengen on 14 June 1985 by Germany, France, Belgium, the Netherlands and Luxembourg.[6]

A Europe that looks back to a long history of warring states and small states has declared its wish to remove the frontiers between the states. The idea of a Europe without frontiers has from the beginning been an idea of freedom: freedom of goods and trade first, but an idea that expanded to include the free movement of people. And it is an idea of freedom because the integration of democratic states strengthens their unity. The absence of internal borders sank such deep roots into the continent's identity that when frontiers were being closed EU Commissioner Avramopoulos issued a warning: 'When Schengen ceases to exist, Europe will die.'[7] Europe without borders is a successful model for an attempt at supra-national collaboration harmonisation and of 'an area of freedom, security and justice', in the frequently quoted phrase from the Treaty of Amsterdam.

But that is only one part of the story. Along with the process of Europeanisation and the dismantling of borders internally, there has been an erection of borders externally. The disappearance of the internal borders makes the external border more prominent.[8] The Dublin Agreement, intended to regulate the competence of the various countries in dealing with asylum applications in the EU,[9] was from the very beginning 'the restrictive shadow on freedom of movement in the Schengen area'.[10] The closeness of the two agreements can be seen from the fact that Articles 28-38 in the Dublin Agreement were simply taken over from Schengen. Two basic ideas of the Dublin Agreement can be identified in them: 'First, asylum seekers in the EU should be assigned to a specific country, which must process their asylum application. Second, they should be given only this one chance to apply for asylum in the Schengen area. Essentially responsibility should lie with the member state that "caused" their entry and thus the asylum application by granting a visa or neglecting to protect the external border.'[11] It is obvious that this arrangement assigns countries in southern Europe responsibility for the asylum process, while countries that are not situated on the EU's external borders (or on borders with few irregular border crossings) can expect hardly any asylum applications. In this logic border states count as the causes of the asylum issue. Because they are unable to protect their borders, they make border crossings possible and are therefore responsible for the applicant for asylum. Why someone seeks asylum is irrelevant in this fixation on administrative acts within the borders. In reality this practice of 'running borders' meant that the system rapidly became overloaded. The reasons included the fact that asylum seekers did not want to be told in advance which country they had to make their asylum application in, the fact that the countries on the borders at first refused to take responsibility for the asylum process, and that only a few transfers (deportations to the country where the border was crossed) were carried out.[12] For these and other reasons the agreement underwent revisions,[13] but the two basic ideas mentioned above were not removed. Even today responsibility for dealing with immigration to Europe lies with the southern European countries, and there is not even a – frequently demanded – quota system to distribute refugees between the member states.

Although the fundamental political idea has remained unchanged since Dublin I, different dominant motives can be identified in the shaping of the border regime. From the beginning securing the border was combined with externalisation strategies. First, in order to secure the Spanish enclaves of Ceuta and Melilla, and then more broadly with the 1995 Barcelona process, West African and North African countries were included in the management of the external borders.[14] Despite numerous difficulties, there followed agreements with Morocco, Libya and finally the most politically significant, with Turkey in May 2016. In return for various benefits, Turkey accepted the obligation to prevent illegal immigrants (especially refugees from Syria) from crossing the border into the EU.[15] Turkey took over the task of securing Europe's borders: the activity of border control was transferred to the other side of the border. In parallel to these strategies of externalisation there was a short-lived phase of humanisation: the shipwreck off Lampedusa in October 2013 with the loss of at least 366 lives marked a turning point in public attitudes, which – reinforced by the Pope's laying of a wreath – (temporarily) changed public discourse and brought the saving of human lives in the Mediterranean into the foreground. Politically this humanisation phase found expression in Mare Nostrum,[16] an Italian naval operation from October 2013 to October 2014 focusing on the rescue of refugees in distress at sea. The peak – and also

67

the end – of the humanisation phase was represented by the acceptance of numerous refugees by Germany and other countries. This so-called refugee crisis revealed a crisis in Europe, the failure of the border regime, since the majority of states did not meet the demands of solidarity.[17]

There was then a further shift in the border regime. The term 'securing' implies that ensuring the security of the borders (and, connected with this, the promise of security for the countries of the EU) becomes more important and will be increasingly attained by military means.[18] An example of this shift is talk about rescue at sea, which in the 'humanitarian phase' was regarded as an obligation, but subsequently increasingly treated as a crime.

The concept of the border expressed in this policy is primarily that of imposing restrictions: the area of freedom and security created inside is defended on the outside. Underlying this is the idea that every sphere of action requires boundaries, including the EU, which seeks by securing its border to protect its capacity for political action – its order. However, when this justified concern is put into practice there are problems. First, in those speeches that evoke the threat to order there is scarcely any evidence that the existing order – and so the capacity for action – is in fact endangered by immigration, and if so, how. Second, there is a fixation on a single border, the external border of the EU, while, as was shown earlier in the symbolic expansion of the concept of a border, (political) action is subject to many limitations. But these diverse limits and restrictions on action are filtered out and the changeability, arbitrariness and stability of borders are ignored in the fixation with the external border.

The path from Schengen to Dublin is far shorter than public opinion believes. For what we described earlier as the formation of a 'European identity', both elements are therefore important, the practices of freedom on the internal borders and defensive measures on the external borders.[19] But it should be noted that there are not two continents, but only one, not the Europe of Schengen and the Europe of Dublin, but just this one Europe, for whose ability to be a convincing peace project we now have cause to fear.

A solution to the moral and political deadlock, which would have to include both dealing with the causes of flight and a fair distribution of refugees across all EU member states, seems, however, impossible in current political circumstances. And in the political cul-de-sac 'A European solution or none at all', a continent persists in passivity.[20]

But even if a European *solution* at the moment seems impossible, the humanitarian crisis demands a European *answer* here and now. As the internal borders fade, the external borders become increasingly visible and a new area for political action opens up. Ironically, the external borders could be not only a part of the problem, but indirectly also create the possibility of a common European answer to the humanitarian crisis.

III Horizontal and vertical borders

As borders between states disappear (on a horizontal level) with the creation of the Schengen area, a new area for political action is created on a vertical level, that is, between the various levels of administration within the member states, but also in relation to the EU as a whole. This area can be occupied by cities, districts and regions. Their historical and geographical characteristics and their proximity to their citizens could make it possible to shape the future of the continent where the humanitarian crisis at its gates has hitherto been mainly administered and so deepened.

These new vertical borders could be imagined in terms suggested by the political scientist Ulrike Guérot:

> In practice we observe no renationalisation, but a splitting of states into different social groups, parties and classes, or regions. Today the City of London is against the industrialised north of England, young people against Wales or Scotland and Northern Ireland against England. Right across Europe the urban population is very often against the countryside or the centre against the regions, the educated and mobile against the less educated and immobile.[21]

Ulrike Guérot here places the emphasis on the divisive effect of these borders, but what appears as a border within the nation states can also connect socio-cultural groups or areas beyond national boundaries if these network on the basis of their structural similarity or shared concerns.

Something like this is happening in the Eurocities network, in which since 1986 European cities have joined forces to develop joint strategies in various fields, such as sustainability, health and the economy, or networks such as CLIP (Cities for Local Integration Policy), which focus on issues of immigration and integration.[22] In addition to this networking by cities and districts, institutional administrative bodies, there is horizontal networking of individuals and groups, who, for example, get involved in social movements. Here areas for action are set up across (national) borders.

If such initiatives are not to produce new forms of discrimination and exclusion, their involvement must be organised on the basis of the principles of subsidiarity and solidarity. This can also ensure that they do not become mere stop-gaps in a failed European policy but – in the best case - are part of a new European vision.[23] Subsidiarity is a fundamental principle of the European Union (Treaty on European Union, Art. 5, para. 3). It regulates rights and duties between vertical bodies. The task of the higher body consists in making possible the independent activity of the lower body where and when – and only there and then – that is necessary. At the same time it has to make sure that it maintains the autonomy of the lower body including by itself withdrawing at the earliest possible moment. 'The principle of subsidiarity thus also has an integrative function…it does not push the weak bodies into surrender, but strengthens them. In so doing it strengthens bottom-up initiatives in relation to top-down approaches.'[24]

The principle of subsidiarity can lead to an exaggeration of the role of lower bodies and a misinterpretation of their autonomy as self-sufficiency. If the cities and regions can't solve the problem, what, if any, is the point of Europe? A Europe of cities and regions can perhaps offer a response to the crisis, but the solution can only come from Europe as a whole, in a combination of vertical and horizontal relationships. Vertically means that the higher levels of the EU not only create space, but also set clear regulations so that autonomy does not become arbitrariness. Horizontally means that subsidiarity – completely in line with Catholic social teaching – must be complemented by solidarity. Solidarity combines, as indicated above, local activities with common action. In the texts of the EU treaties, most of all the Lisbon treaty, solidarity is mentioned as a fundamental value put into practice by 'enhanced cooperation'. The borders between Barcelona and Berlin or Savoy and Bohemia transcend the concept of demarcation: commonalities such as 'major European city' or 'European region' make it possible to act in solidarity across national frontiers.

Unfortunately this solidarity is largely an ideal, since this cooperation is what is often missing – not only in immigration policy, but especially there and in the related border regulations. Solidarity requires being aware of the rights and interests of others and taking them into account instead of pursuing (only) national interests and taking common action on this basis. When this does not happen within the EU, new frontiers are created between the member states.

IV Conclusion

We mentioned at the beginning of this article how far our approach to its subject would be influenced by current events. As the first wave of the pandemic in Europe unfolded in June 2020 there have once more been signs of an astonishing change in attitudes to borders: 'Precisely at the moment when we were not allowed to leave our homes, we became more cosmopolitan than ever before.'[25] At the moment at which all states were battling comparable problems, citizens and politicians carefully followed the decisions of other states and compared them. Different situations were noted, and politicians gave interviews to the media of other European states. While for about three months barriers came down again at the internal borders, it began to be widely accepted that a return to the time 'before Schengen' was not desirable. And that was not all. Possibly a new form of dismantling borders had begun, which embodies possibilities of solidarity that could be put into practice, for example, in the negotiations over the gigantic financing programme *Next Generation EU*.[26] Time will tell.

Translated by Francis McDonagh

Notes

1. Vasilis Tsianos in conversation with Axel Rahmlow, 'Die Lager müssen sofort evakuiert werden': https://www.deutschlandfunkkultur.de/corona-und-die-fluechtlinge-in-griechenland-die-lager.1008.de.html?dram:article_id=473002 (Accessed 09/12/20).
2. Michel Foucault , 'Préface à la transgression', *Critique*, no 195-196: Hommage à G. Bataille,' *Dits et Écrits* I (Paris, 1994) , pp 233-268, quotation from p. 237.
3. See Kleinschmidt, 'Semantik der Grenze', in APUZ 4-5/2014: https://www.bpb.de/apuz/176297/semantik-der-grenze?p=all (Accessed 13/12/2020).
4. See Sabine Hess and Bernd Kasparek (ed.), *Grenzregime. Diskurse, Praktiken, Institutionen in Europa*, Berlin, 2012; Vassilis S. Tsianos and Bernd Kasparek, 'Zur Krise

des europäischen Grenzregimes: eine regimetheoretische Annäherung, Widersprüche'. *Verlag Westfälisches Dampfboot*, vol. 138, 35 (2015), No. 4, 8-22.

5. 'Agreement between the Governments of the States of the Benelux Economic Union, the Federal Republic of Germany and the French Republic on the gradual abolition of checks at their common borders': https://eur-lex.europa.eu/legal-content/EN/TXT/HTML/?uri=CELEX:42000A0922(01)&from=EN

6. The agreement is also known as the Schengen *acquis* or Schengen I. The implementation of these still very vague ideas followed in the 1990 Schengen Convention. Although historically and logically it precedes the Dublin Agreement, it was in fact signed four days afterwards, on 15 June 1990. The Schengen Convention came into force on 1 September 1993, except for some sections, which did not come into force until 1995.

7. See Andrea Dernbach, 'Ohne Schengen hört Europa auf zu existieren', *Der Tagesspiegel*, https://www.tagesspiegel.de/politik/eu-kommissar-gegen-grenzkontrollen-ohne-schengen-hoert-europa-auf-zu-existieren/24198584.html.ee (Accessed 14/12/20200).

8. See Sabine Hess and Bernd Kasparek, 'Under Control? Or Border (as) Conflict: Reflections on the European Border Regime', *Social Inclusion*, vol. 5 (2017), Issue 3, 58–68: 60.

9. The Dublin Agreement was signed by twelve countries on 15 June 1990 and came into force in September 1997. Because of the United Kingdom's departure from the EU, it will no longer be part of the Agreement from January 2021.

10. David Lorenz, 'Von Dublin-Domino bis Kirchenasyl. Kämpfe um Dublin III', in: *Movements. Journal für kritische Migrations- und Grenzregimeforschung* 2015 1 (1), 2.

11. David Lorenz, 'Von Dublin-Domino bis Kirchenasyl', 1.

12. See Lorenz, 'Von Dublin-Domino bis Kirchenasyl', 2.

13. The Dublin II Regulation (2003) and the Dublin III Regulation further develop Dublin I and replace it.

14. See Hess and Kasparek, 'Under Control', 55.

15. See European Council, *EU-Turkey statement, 18 March 2016* (Press release): https://www.consilium.europa.eu/en/press/press-releases/2016/03/18/eu-turkey-statement/ (Accessed 14/12/20).

16. See Hess and Kasparek, 'Under Control', 59-60.

17. On 2 April 2020 the European Court decided that three countries that completely refused to accept refugees had broken EU law.

18. See Hess/ Kasparek, 'Under Control', 61-62.

19. See Tobias Heinze, Sebastian Illigens and Michael Pollock, *Doing Frontiers: On the Performativity of the European Border and Migration Regime*, DNGPS Working Paper, Osnabrück, 2016, 1-16: https://www.academia.edu/26396879/Doing_Frontiers_On_the_Performativity_of_the_European_Border_and_Migration_Regime_DNGPS_Working_Papers_2016_ (Accessed 15/12/2020).

20. In March 2020 the situation reached crisis point. Greece suspended the right to asylum: asylum applications were not allowed, and people were returned to Turkey. On Europe's external border order was suspended because its basis, the Dublin Convention, unduly burdened particular states and so was unjust, and because there is disunity between the countries about what they think the EU stands for.

21. Ulrike Guérot, 'Europa zwischen Geist und Ungeist. Nationalismus und Konzepte europäischer Föderation in historischer Perspektive. Antrittsvorlesung an der Donauuniversität', *Wiener Zeitung*, 28.04.2017 : https://www.wienerzeitung.at/

nachrichten/politik/europa/888978_Europa-zwischen-Geist-und-Ungeist.-Nationalismus-und-Konzepte-europaeischer-Foederation-in-historischer-Perspektive.html?em_no_split=1 (Accessed 15/12/2020).

22. Whereas only 40 cities are members of CLIP, in Germany (as at March 2020) 141 cities are 'safe havens', that is, they have declared their willingness to make a contribution to the safe arrival of refugees. See https://seebruecke.org (Accessed 15/12/20). Horizontal networking also takes place within states.

23. A proposal for such a vision was put forward by Ulrike Guérnot and Robert Menasse in 2013 and they have continued to develop it. See Ulrike Guérot and Robert Menasse, 'Manifest für die Begründung einer Europäischen Republik', *Die Presse,* 23.03.2013: https://www.diepresse.com/1379843/manifest-fur-die-begrundung-einer-europaischen-republik (Accessed 15/12/2020).

24. Norbert Brieskorn, Art. 'Subsidiarität', *Enzyklopädie zur Rechtsphilosophie*, II.5,4: http://www.enzyklopaedie-rechtsphilosophie.net/inhaltsverzeichnis/19-beitraege/81-subsidiartaet (Accessed 15/12/2020).

25. Ivan Krastev, 'Das Ende der Heuchelei', Interview, *Die Zeit*, 10.06.2020, 4.

26. 750,000 million euros were to be allocated for innovations in individual regions and to strengthen the EU project. See European Commission, *Speech by President von der Leyen at the event 'Progettiamo il Rilancio'* 13 June 2020: https://ec.europa.eu/commission/presscorner/detail/en/speech_20_1060 (Accessed 16/12/2020).

The (Christian?) Future of Europe

CETTINA MILITELLO

Is there any sense in talking about Europe? About its future? If the answer is 'yes', it is necessary to discuss its transient borders and put them aside, opening oneself to the values of transculturality. Given the phenomenon of migration which is changing the face of Europe, this is a discourse of the utmost urgency, all while a profound identity crisis is assaulting its values, models and institutions. This crisis is impacting the Churches and makes one fear whether they will be able to overcome it. We need new starts, to "invest the good news with a new meaning", making it capable of questioning; to rebuild the "relationship", demonstrating it in its immediate obviousness. I would reject the pretentious idea of "Christian" Europe – which, perhaps, there has never been – to focus instead on the re-invention of micro-communities, the yeast of a new world. They would contribute to the future of "this" Europe by identifying and promoting a new anthropological, social, political, economic, environmental paradigm, marked by subsidiarity, by mutuality, by inter-relatedness and by dialogue.

I will be forgiven for not entering into the merits of the significant literature about the so-called "Christian roots" and for leaving to one side the diatribe about secularisation, the final consequence – or not – of the "Christian" separation between the religious and public sphere.[1] And forgive me once again if I do not appeal to the *skyline*, to the configuration of the European cities where towers, domes and bell-towers stand out, different in shape, but, in their magnificence, all full of identity values.

It is easy to articulate the story and to project onto one or other model of Christianity even the *arché* of the idea of Europe. Again it is easy to see it

74

as a geo-political category. But, thinking carefully about it, Europe, even geographically, is an abstraction, given that it is one with what we would rightly call at best Eurasia, or even Afro-Eurasia. In fact Europe – and it is a myth – came to birth in the crucible of the Mediterranean, a happy poetic invention which personalises the love of Zeus for a young girl, Europa, seduced by him assuming the appearance of a bull. The myth is a sort of aetiology about some Mediterranean peoples; in this particular case, the inhabitants of Crete, who would give name of the young girl, who had become their queen, to the territory which lay beyond the sea to the north of the island. Already there is approximation in the myth.

Whatever its hinterland – Mediterranean, I would say – from the lands which emerged from the Atlantic coasts (and the islands close to them) to the mountain chain of the Urals there was a desire to draw a space marked by the name Europe. A very diverse area from an ethnic perspective: a multitude of peoples followed on from each other, mixing with each other, acquiring and/or maintaining their own features, irreducibly their own, which still emerge today despite the so-called national boundaries.

This crucible was considered a unity. And again myth, in other forms, fed this presumption. In fact there was never a unity which was truly such: different values, models, institutions have marked the history of the peoples who inhabited it. So much so that, rightly, we can ask ourselves whether it makes sense to speak about Europe or whether, in speaking about it, we must necessarily reduce or enlarge its borders, or even reject them. East, West, North, South acquire their own characteristics. Nor does the South end at the southern coast of the Mediterranean, given that the same northern coast of Africa is in some way European, just like the extremes of Asia which face onto the same sea. Suffice to think of the events of Santa Sofia which send us into crisis, in the past and in the present.

Faced with these problems, which are anything but slight, how can we speak about the Europe of the future, and how can we ask what importance the Christian faith will still have in it?

I What is the future for Europe?
Faced with the paths of unification it is difficult to distinguish its authentic and profound dynamics: even when clothed in idealism, they often have dominant projects behind them. If this was obvious in the past, it is also

75

so in the present. European unity is seen more as an economic opportunity than a socio-political process of union and exchange between the peoples who live there. Of course at the beginning, in the minds of the founders, there was the desire to put an end to the conflicts which from the middle of the twentieth century brought bloodshed to the continent (and beyond). The idea of solidarity between peoples, fraternity starting out from common values, first of all the state of law and therefore the same respect for citizens, all equal bearers of inalienable rights and duties, seemed to drive out fratricidal conflict. But beyond hearing about being "strong and free" there lies once again the idea of a wider market, aimed at promoting the advantage of one over the other. Paradoxically – but this belongs to the paradox of being human – economic unification preceded and precedes political unification. The latter, though far from materialising, nevertheless availed itself of a high-ranking bureaucracy, whose complex mechanisms certainly did not help to make a united Europe a proximate and living experience, a "community", as it was in the plan of the founding fathers. Nor have economic concerns succeeded in overcoming national interests, in the name of which very harsh conditions have been imposed on States far from the *standard* of the efficiency of the countries considered economically virtuous.

United Europe has thus become the Europe of suspicion, of the privileged axes, of the *leader* nations, to the point of the foolish multiplication of the member states, the last of which, what is more, became interpreters of a national-populist vision. The new, broader markets did not produce the desired effects: if anything, they increased new walls and fences. This is without mentioning the politically-constituted backwards step of having given decision-making power to the Council, which comprises all the States, weakening the supranationality of the European Commission, thus favouring the "stronger" states. Nor was the humiliation about the "European constitution", deferred to better times.

It is clear that we will not proceed far along this path, and Brexit is its most striking expression. So, it is necessary either to agree on the inconsistency of the European plan, or ask questions about the choices made or to be made in the future.

Perhaps the future of Europe needs a profound re-thinking. The national States must cede an appropriate part of their sovereignty. The European

Community, in the twenty-seven states which already comprise it, must speak an identical language at the level of foreign, economic, and health policy, the same language of civil rights, employment, immigration, and so forth. Hence it is necessary to really think about a confederation, governed by an elective democracy, whose leaders have effective decision-making power. Within it, regional details would be respected. The national States, which are the fruits of unintentional and summary processes of unification, are marked internally by profound divisions. Often even the common language is at stake. More generally there is not a national culture, but a multiplicity of regional cultures, the fruit of that settling which placed immigrant and native populations together in region after region.

Yes, because Europe (and not just Europe) has always been a place of the dynamics of migration. From the north towards the south and the south towards the north, from the east towards the west and the west towards the east, its history is that of a continuous turnover of subjects, who then find their equilibrium, but never deny their cultural specificity. Very often, before the national States and their unification processes, the different regions constituted autonomous and diversified political entities. An example of this is Italy, and it owes to this diversity the unique superabundance of its cultural assets.

This atavistic awareness remains. And while it peculiarly characterises the map of the continent in its geographic completeness, beyond the boundaries of sea and mountains it throws it into disorder if it opens to us what lies beyond: a not incoherent but, dare we say, 'symmetrical' other.

Yes, Europe's boundaries are transient. What does a non-European citizen of Istanbul, a citizen of Israel, or one of the states of the Near East or of North Africa do? Isn't it perhaps by visiting them that one discovers how a single civilisation brought them together, in a cosmopolitan, inter-religious and inter-cultural mix, which, come to think of it, spoiled only by the boorish colonialism of the twentieth century (and then, following the Second World War, the nonchalant division of the world by pencil strokes)? The caesura is much closer to us, time-wise, I would say, than we would like to think. And we experience the whole drama: think of the powder-keg of the Middle East, the rise of fundamentalism, phenomena nourished by the culture medium of an arrogant and uneducated colonialism, blind even to cultural discernment.

If Europe has a future it is therefore that of discussing transient borders, of putting them aside, opening oneself again to the currents which generated and changed it and recognising oneself as equal to them in the values of transculturality. In fact only when they have really been absorbed can Europe be great. As an outstanding workshop of the encounter of people and cultures, the native place of democracy as recognition of the equality of citizens' rights and duties, then I would say it is a victor, culturally speaking, when it has accepted new peoples, blending with them, receiving their gifts and in turn giving the great capacity to welcome and make its own that which at first appeared to it as foreign or even hostile.

This is an absolutely urgent discourse at a time when the unparalleled phenomenon of migration is destined to change the face of Europe. Never as in this moment has everything been gambled on the capacity to welcome and dialogue as equals. There is no "superior" European culture discombobulated by North African or Asian "poor" driven to us by hunger and war. There is a challenge to the witness of a common humanity which goes beyond language, beyond one's own culture, always open to bold transculturations.

But all this takes place while the West is experiencing its most profound crisis: a crisis of identity, crisis of faith, crisis of values, crisis of models, crisis of institutions. The fall in the birth rate, where it reaches and goes below zero, is an obvious confirmation of a problem which makes no room for the future. Nor is the birth rate attributable just to choice. Bodies themselves become infertile when besieged by tedium and by the vagueness of the present to the point that they no longer hope in a future. And yet there are so many very good resources: think alone of cultural patrimony, either of language and tradition, or works of art, or utopian expectations.

But the prevailing expectation is that all this is no longer enough. Europe is feeling old; it is old and does not understand who will restore its vigour.

II A Christian future?
The crisis impacts the Churches and is so profound that one fears whether they will be able to overcome it. And it impacts all of them, whatever the denomination, as proven by the departure of so many from the so-called "historic" Churches. At the Roman Catholic level, it impacts the values,

78

models, and above all demonstrates the inadequacy of the institution in making room for emerging values and subsequent models. The institution is then seen as a mess of opposition, aimed at ensuring nothing changes, as if the future were guaranteed by immobility. One's own privilege is defended, fiercely engaging oneself so that power remains in the hands of the people in charge of the institutions themselves. Only in this way can we explain the peculiar arguments aimed at perpetuating gender asymmetry and hierarchological myopia. A Church which dares to do without women has no future. Nor is the disjointed research about acrobatic forms of presence sufficient: it is in effect irrelevant if it does not unravel the question of ministry. A Church which, despite Vatican II, insists in the inequality of its members; which does not renounce the juxtaposition between leaders and subjects; which despite appeals to "go out" remains sheltered in defence, has no future.

On the other hand, it is very obvious that change is missing. Communities remain deprived of contacts. In a fight to the death they are drawn together as if re-drawing the map were enough to enliven them. In the meantime tasks which in fact do not guarantee correspondence between ministry and charism have been entrusted to those who are inadequate. Those in charge, bishops, vicars "in movement" whose *identikit* seems to be rather that of *manager*, committed as they are to administer the economy rather than to "serve" – *diakonein* – the community of faithful.

It seems a panacea to return to a past which never existed. Hence the regret for the "sacred", the re-launch of obsolete forms, the claim for an ontological difference between the baptised and the ordained, which characterises and divides the people of God, once again extinguishing its subjectivity and prophecy.

The Covid-19 pandemic set before us a clerical delusion, in the shape of superstitions about living the faith. Media exposure prevailed, and the virtual clumsily replaced a relationship, a closeness to the other person, which was already in crisis.

The pandemic laid bare a situation which is now unsustainable. What was noticed – and I am speaking above all about Italy – was the inability to grasp the *kairos*, to make it, beyond the rhetoric, a "real" re-starting point, discarding all that offends common sense and the essential nature of the Gospel. And that requires a radical reform.

Above all it must mark the end of denominational divisions. It is time for mutual recognition between Christians and to think about how to unite their strengths not out of self-interest but in order to speak to ourselves and to the world about the desire and capacity to be daring about the future. This means that the Roman Catholic Church must cast off its premise of a Catholicity exclusively its own, while the Church in the multiple concreteness of the place in which it is incarnate is holy, catholic and apostolic. Catholic is inherent to the Churches; in all and in each it is present in its entirety, beyond and despite the innumerable divisions in the course of history.

In Roman Catholic circles, but the suggestion goes beyond the denominational boundary, there is so much talk of "synodality". But that presupposes overcoming the clerical-lay opposition and the radical abandonment of any gender discrimination. Without these two prior conditions, synodality remains an empty, deceitful term, beyond any "Christian" logic. Communities cannot start out again if they do not regain awareness of being people of God on the move, a people of brothers and sisters, who, each marked by the gift poured out upon them by the Spirit, working in synergy, witness to the radical nature of God's kingdom. Thus they undertake to discern signs in the present and act as a consequence, becoming companions of suffering humanity. The Church/Churches as a people of solidarity, the Exodus, de-clericalised, de-hierachicalised, decentralised, and multi-cultural, at the service of those who are part of it and those who are or remain outside it. The Church/Churches as critical conscience in the face of unsustainable development, of mother earth abused and exploited. The Church/Churches as a strong voice which makes their own the cry of the abused and marginalised, claiming their full humanity and promoting positive actions of awareness and liberation. But that cannot happen without a serious re-thinking of the institution which must return to being simple, essential, functional to the proclamation, the praise, the co-responsibility which marks everyone, without any exceptions.

It is not just about a "political" choice as if the resource were the democratisation of the Church as well, a positioning of it to one or other side in the theatre of a world otherwise divided and perpetually in conflict. It is about appealing to "expertise", in other words to the charism of each person. Synodality is truly such a thing, within the intertwining of expertise, in communal discernment, a discernment of the symphonic plurality of ministries in the local communities, of the symphonic plurality of the particular Churches, of the symphonic plurality of the cultures which they inhabit; a discernment and consequent and coherent operability: it is utopia, the impetus of renewal. Nor is it an irrelevant proposal, not even for anyone who by now considers all public value of faith to be irrelevant.

II Start again from where?

New starts should be invented, to eliminate courageously inauthentic and unacceptable experiences. There is a need to "invest with new meaning" the good news, to make it attractive, seductive, capable of questioning and changing those who now see salvation in the immediate satisfaction of their personal and most private needs. There is a need to rebuild the "relationship", to demonstrate it in its immediate obviousness.

I believe that the Christian paradigm, thinking of (and seeing) the Church as body in the synergy of the different members might still suggest something.

In the immediate future I would reject the pretentious idea of "Christian" Europe – which perhaps has never been – to focus instead on the re-invention of micro-communities which become the yeast of a new world, conscious of the aberrations into which the Church, too, has fallen. For their part they would contribute to the future of "this" Europe by identifying and promoting a new anthropological, social, political, economic, environmental paradigm. A Europe which is truly "community", and marked therefore by subsidiarity, mutuality and inter-relatedness.

It would be sufficient to invest with new meaning, in other words make forthcoming, comprehensible, and effective, the heart of Christian dogma: the mystery of a God who is Trinity of Persons, the mystery of a God who became flesh and makes us his body. The flesh, the body – the becoming flesh of God in Jesus of Nazareth – are the paradigm from where to start again in the immediacy of a reconciled relationship of ourselves to ourselves, of ourselves to others.

The requirement of the future is that of a "new" encounter of peoples and cultures. Others will bring new nourishment to the old continent. The Europe of the future is multicultural. To experience this with purpose, with no regrets about the past and no fears for the future, it is necessary to accept the challenge of a supportive humanity, despite differences; in fact, to start from the differences. Otherness is not "hell" but "the" resource; it is so in the complex variety of variations which comprise it and to the extent that it makes room for "gratuitousness" as its original statute.

Of course new transcultural incentives could come from religious suggestions, too, shared or not since the dawn of time. For example, recourse to the category of "mercy" could open us to a fruitful dialogue between the different faiths which now characterise those who live in Europe; and, besides the religious experience itself, it could focus a different attention on the human person and on the intrinsic limitation which constitutes the person, fragile and pilgrim as he or she is in the polarity of birth and the inevitability of death.

Perhaps, and this, too, has transcultural and trans-religious implications, one could – and this is the proposal of Pope Francis – start again from the category of brotherhood/sisterhood. Such a category must be purified of the residual implications of a "patriarchal" kind.

I want a Europe which is capable of attesting to the value of the other and of devoting oneself so that nothing and no-one thinks of denying it. All the Christian communities, without triumphalism and without powerful collateral, could become the yeast of a new culture which knows how to knead and get its hands dirty in the fraternal, friendly encounter, aware of being not the end but a means, seen in gospel terms a "sign" of the intimate union with God and of the unity of all in the human race.

Translated by Patricia and Liam Kelly

Notes

1. *Per la convivenza tra i popoli oltre il razzismo e la tolleranza*, Vita e pensiero, Milan 1993. Sandro Fontana (ed.)., *Il futuro dell'Europa*, Marsilio, Venice 1996; Markus Vogt and Sarah Numico (eds), *Salvaguardia del creato e sviluppo sostenibile: orizzonti per le Chiese in Europa*, Gregoriana Libreria Editrice, Padua 2007; Manuel Alejandro Rodríguez de la Peña y Francisco Javier López Atanes (eds), Traditio Catholica. *En torno a las raíces cristianas de Europa*, CEU Ediciones, Madrid 2009; Autiero Antonio and Perroni Marinella (eds.), La Bibbia nella storia d'Europa. Dalle divisioni all'incontro, EDB, Bologna 2012; Javier Maria Prades López, 'Una antropología en acción para el futuro de Europa', *Scripta Theologica* 47 (2015), 293-310; Evert Van de Poll, *Europe and the Gospel! Influences, Developments, Mission Challenges.* Master Class Edition, Heerde, Schuman Centre for European Studies, 2016; Gaetano Castello and Carmine Mattarrazzo (edd.), *Per un nuovo umanesimo*, Il pozzo di Giacobbe, Trapani 2017; Ramón Jáuregui Atondo, 'El futuro de Europa (o más bien la Europa del futuro)', *Revista de Fomento Social* 73/1 (2018), 65-90; Olivier Roy, *L'Europa è ancora cristiana?*, Feltrinelli, Milan 2019; COMECE, *Ricostruire comunità in Europa*, in Regno-doc 7/2019; Riflessioni sul futuro dell'Europa, eds Alessandro Gennaro and Rainer Stefano Masera, Aracne, Rome 2020.

We the (Catholic) People:
Is Populism Hijacking Christianity? An
Eastern European Perspective

ZORAN GROZDANOV

The rise of the populist movements in Eastern Europe is heavily supported by the religious arguments that cause division between "us" and "them", between cultures and religious traditions. During the struggles for the formation of nation-states in the 1990s and during the renaissance of national movements in the 1970s and 1980s, encyclicals of John Paul II strongly reverberated in Eastern Catholic countries that share a Catholic identity. In this article, we are trying to elaborate on the fact that populist movements, particulary in the Croatian context, use the vocabulary and concepts that gained their theological support in the writings of prominent religious leaders and thinkers. Strong emphasis on patria, *ethnic and cultural belonging, that was supported by key Christian doctrines such as the Incarnation, gave religious fuel to patriotism and nationalism in the 1990s and continues to influence present populist movements.*

Most Christian academic texts, reviews, and newspaper articles that write on the dangers of current populist processes complain that populist movements and leaders misuse religion in their theories and practices. In that sense, we can read that populists 'hijack' the (Christian) religion, 'distort' it, 'co-opt' it, and, finally, that populism "is contrary to faith and doctrine and inimical to the life of communion and community."[1] To someone not very well versed in the nuances of faith and doctrine, nor in the history of various theological traditions, Christianity may seem like a young, innocent bride seduced by a manipulative and crafty groom who, clad in an elegant suit, promises her a bright future. He approaches her, robbing her of her resources, and morphing her into something she isn't. Is this story of innocence on the part of the Church and craftiness on the side of populism true? Is Christianity a mere excellent platform for populists, one that does not want to be trapped by populist claims of a strong national identity, of identities divided by ethnic or cultural belonging, and of its defence of some sort of values that it declares to be Christian? Or, is there something inherent in Christianity that provokes the populist to take it and mobilize it for its own agenda?

These questions are yet to be explored, as most texts about the relationship between populism and religion discuss the populist hijacking of religion, claiming it corrupts Christianity's true nature by insisting on a sharp boundary between 'us' and 'them', and a sharp distinction between cultures, ethnic belongings, etc. The roots and resources from which populists derive the material for their agendas depend heavily on their social context, which is why, as Jan Werner Müller writes, populism is hard to define.[2] The reason why populists spread fear may depend on some economic, religious, cultural, or ethnic 'other', where this 'other' varies from one context to another. Since it is difficult to define or articulate one distinctive populist pattern, this article, for the sake of brevity, describes possible resources for populist agendas in Eastern and Southeast Europe, which stem from the very heart of the Church. More specifically, these resources stem from its – if unofficial – teaching: from the teaching of Pope John Paul II on cultural identity, patriotism, the concept of the people (*populus*), the homeland and especially on their reappropriation in the context of Eastern Europe.

The relationship between Christian theological resources and the rise of populism is, as we have said, under-explored, which is why some readers could be surprised by seeing John Paul II mentioned in the context of populist agendas. That surprise might be augmented by John Paul's explicit views against nationalism and against exclusions based on one's belonging of any kind, which he had consistently attacked, most prominently in his book *Memory and Identity,*[3] which was published after his death. Given this overt stance against nationalism, one would rightfully wonder what the late Pope has to do with populism. Due to the limited scope of this text, we limit ourselves to asking some questions and posing an initial thesis for exploring the theological resources that might have contributed to the rise of populism.

There are various kinds of populism, ranging from its left-wing versions, as exemplified by the Syriza and Podemos movements and parties, to its right-wing expressions, such as Prawo i Sprawiedliwość (Law and Justice) in Poland, FIDESZ in Hungary, AfD and PEGIDA in Germany, and certain Croatian NGOs.[4] Since we are dealing with the Eastern European context, we will focus on right-wing populism whose identity politics heavily rely on ethnic, cultural, and religious belonging. This interplay between various belongings, as Miščević notes, depends on the immediate social context, which, in turn, depends on the role of ethnic and national belonging in the history of particular state. So, for instance, if a country "in which the nationalist tradition is being shunned for its historical effects... the project will give birth to populisms that are not so much nationalistic, but rather turn to cultural, religious identities, *e.g.,* Christianity/Islam contrast."[5] If, on the other hand, a country has an overt nationalist tradition – which is a spectrum that includes most Eastern European countries – its populisms will be nationalist, relying on ethnic elements, and, in this sense, on cultural and even religious customs that stem from ethnic belonging.

Right-wing populisms do not merely endorse overt nationalism. They also rely on patriotic sentiments and rhetoric.[6] A patriotism that relies on a shared national culture and language is a topic where John Paul II's thought heavily influenced theologians in countries that had struggled for national independence. As early as 1981, in his encyclical *Laborem excercens*, the late Pope clearly states: "man combines his deepest human identity with membership in a nation."[7] The term 'nation' appears to be the most significant concept within his elaboration of 'the deepest human identity', since he gives it a theological foundation. For the Pope, our nation, culture, and, as the primary group where we develop our identities, our family, stem from the nature of the Incarnation,[8] where he identifies the theological dimension of the Incarnation with the concrete human being. When speaking of the Incarnation, he says: "We are not dealing here with the 'abstract' man, but the real, 'concrete', 'historical' man[9] The concreteness and historicity of the human being are, for him, defined by the shared culture, shared history, and shared language where this person flourishes and receives their identity. Building on this thesis, John Paul II develops a theology of nation and culture that is entirely in line with the Romantic vision of *Volksgeist*,[10] 'the spirit of the nation', which is characteristic of every single nation, and its homeland as a primary resource for the building of the nation. Speaking of the concept of the homeland, he says that there is "a deep connection between the spiritual and the material aspect, between culture and territory. The territory that is usurped from one nation by force, in a certain sense, becomes a plea, a cry addressed to the 'spirit' of the nation itself."[11]

The late Pope, speaking from his Polish perspective, which is marked primarily by the program of building a nation-state, prioritizes the concept of 'patriotism', which he relates directly to the spiritual heritage dominant in the formation of a specific nation. He even ties it to Jesus himself, for whom he says, his "message contains the deepest elements of the theological vision of homeland and culture."[12] Although he puts very high value on the concept of patriotism and nation, he unambiguously condemns nationalism. John Paul II understood nationalism as imperialist, chauvinistic, and exclusionary project. In that sense, we cannot call him a nationalist pope, nor a populist one.

On the other hand, as we have seen, he highly appreciated the *patria*, the concept of a homeland, and the idea of nation intimately connected to the territory out of which the state emerges. Moreover, he linked these concepts to the event of the Incarnation, providing a theological foundation for basing our identity on something that is shared by only one group of people in our multicultural world. His concepts found fertile soil in Eastern European countries, which bore traditional Catholic cultures and had a legacy of nationalist politics. This fact is not only very sensitive ground for the theological foundation of populist and nationalist movements that rely on the concept of the 'people' (morally defined as members of a particular culture, ethnic group, or religious belonging) but also for understanding the Church's mission in the contemporary world. As research on the rise of religious voices in Yugoslavia before the fall of the Berlin wall confirms, "if the Church is naturally rooted in every single people and every single nation… the result is that the Church has to be nationally oriented, which also means that she has to be oriented in a national-political way".[13]

Conclusion

Where does this short introduction into the possible links between late Pope's evaluation of the role of the culture, nation and ethnic belonging lead us in discussing contemporary populistic agendas? For one, the context of Eastern Europe is in a constant struggle between acceptance of the liberal democratic traditions that relativize influence of the particular ethnic or religious identities on political decision-making and its faithfulness to the religious and ethnic traditions upon which politics should be guided. The reason why most of the countries in the former Eastern block are attached to their ethnic and religious traditions certainly lies in the fact that those were the resources that led those same countries to the achievement of their national states and formation of their identities before and after the fall of the Berlin wall.[14] In such context we can also read efforts of John Paul II who gives huge relevance to religious belonging for the formation of particular cultural, ethnic and national identities – those identities that are still struggling to form into the nation-state and in which the Church was one of the foundational institutions that carried cultural and ethnic identity during the centuries of historical turmoil.

Identities that arose from these strong affiliations of religious, cultural and national identities have gained their momentum in recent populist claims against immigrations, but also in populist agendas in which the politics that should be performed in the countries that have strong Catholic legacy should be guided by the tradition of particular country.[15] These traditions have their roots in religious reasoning which in the front of the political decision-making prioritizes cultural and ethnic belonging and not citizenship and respect for human rights.

Notes

1. See Editorial in *Concilium* 2 (2019), Th.-M. Courau, S. Abraham, and M. Babić (ed.), *Populism and Religion*, 8.
2. Jan Werner Müller, *Što je populizam?*, Zagreb, Tim Press, 15. (Croatian translation, in English, *What is Populism?*, Philadelphia, University of Pennsylvania Press, 2016.)
3. Ivan Pavao II, *Sjećanje i identitet: Razgovori na prijelazu tisućljeća*, Split: Verbum, 2005 (I quoted here from the Croatian translation. English translation is available as *Memory and Identity: Conversations at the Dawn of a Millenium*, Rizzoli, 2005).

4. For an overview of the broad spectrum of populism, see Nenad Miščević, "Populism and Nationalism," in Violeta Beširević (ed.), *New Politics of Decisionism*, The Hague, Eleven International Publishing, 2019., 61-90, esp. 63-64; Pierre-André Taguieff, *Osveta nacionalizma: Neopopulisti i ksenofobi u napadu na Europu*, Zagreb, Tim press, 2017. (Croatian translation. French original *La revanche du nationalisme: Néopopulistes et xénophobes á l'assaut de l'Europe*, Paris, Presses Universitaires de France, 2015).

5. See Miščević, op. cit., 69.

6. The difference between nationalism and patriotism is highly contested, primarily with regard to the definition of patriotism. Within the Eastern European context, speaking in general terms, patriotism is intimately connected with love for one's country, which is perceived primarily as a 'nation-state', so we can speak of love for one's majority culture, ethnicity, language, etc. An excellent examination of patriotism and nationalism as -isms with very similar resources for defining one's identity can be found in Stephen Backhouse's article, "Nationalism and Patriotism," in Nicholas Adams, George Pattison, and Graham Ward (ed.), *The Oxford Handbook of Theology and Modern European Thought*, London-New York, Oxford University Press, 2013, 41-60, esp. 46 where he writes: "By telling you who you are and what you should love, patriotic narratives make overarching identity claims along similar lines to nationalism."

7. John Paul II, *Laborem exercens*, http://www.vatican.va/content/john-paul-ii/en/encyclicals/documents/hf_jp-ii_enc_14091981_laborem-exercens.html, §10.

8. I have further elaborated on the relationship between Incarnation and identity in the formation of national identities in John Paul II, in Zoran Grozdanov, „From Incarnation to Identity: The Theological Background of National-Populist Politics in the Balkans", in Joshua Ralston and Ulrich Schmiedel (ed.), *The Spirit of Populism: Political Theologies in Polarized Times*, Leiden: Brill, 2021 (forthcoming)

9. John Paul II, *Redemptor hominis*, http://www.vatican.va/content/john-paul-ii/en/encyclicals/documents/hf_jp-ii_enc_04031979_redemptor-hominis.html, §13.

10. See Dorian Llywelyn, *Toward a Catholic Theology of Nationality*, Lanham: Rowman and Littlefield, 2010, 164.

11. Ivan Pavao II, *Sjećanje i identitet*, 65.

12. *Sjećanje i identitet*, 66

13. Darko Hudelist, *Rim, a ne Beograd: Promjena doba i mirna ofenziva Katoličke crkve u Hrvatskoj u Titovoj SFR Jugoslaviji (1975.-1984.)* (*Rome and not Belgrade: The Transformation of Ages and the Peaceful Offensive of the Catholic Church in Croatia in Tito's Yugoslavia (1975-1984)*, Zagreb: Alfa, 2017., 233.

14. On the role of the religious traditions in the formation of nation-states, see Vjekoslav Perica, *Balkan Idols*: *Religion and Nationalism in Yugoslav States*, New York: Oxford University Press, 2002.

15. See, for instance, recent debates on the rights of Serbian minority in Croatia, https://balkaninsight.com/2015/06/15/croatian-politicians-fuelling-hatred-of-serbs/ (accessed 27 October 2020).

The Mediterranean as a Space of Inter-cultural Recognition

VALERIO CORRADI

The analysis of the geopolitical dynamics which run through the Mediterranean highlights the significance of the challenge of recognition. The peoples, regions, cities and cultures of the Mediterranean area suffer from the absence or weakening of the processes of recognition of their own identity and dignity which are essential for the construction of ways of dialogue and affinity. It is necessary to go beyond the cultural non-recognition which is generating frustration, resentment and feelings of oppression and exclusion and return to the originating idea of "mediterraneus" as a space found between the different lands, peoples and cultures, acting as mediator between them

I A many-sided and ever-moving context
The Mediterranean is a place of encounter and the search for the balance between different geographic and cultural worlds, which throughout history have been often opposed but also capable of surprising outbursts of solidarity. After the apparent loss of importance recorded in recent centuries, today the Mediterranean appears to be an environment in which we can see the many-sided effects of the process of globalisation, which here has given rise to interests and questions which simultaneously impact upon the social, political, religious and economic spheres. As a result the Mediterranean area appears to be an area to experiment with the possible outcomes of conflicts and forms of instability which are affected by the events within the various regions which overlook it, from Europe to the Middle East, and Africa. At the same time it has become the place where

we measure ourselves against the main forms of contemporary human mobility, comprising, on the one hand, the dreaded flow of migration, and, on the other, the so-much sought after and desired flow of tourists. The affinity between different ethnic, religious and denominational groups has kept the Mediterranean in a chronic state of crisis which every so often intensifies, giving rise to real and proper conflicts. This interweaving of divergent and convergent processes and of multiplicity and unity which characterise the "Mediterranean nature"[1] has been masterfully captured and described by authors with very different approaches and sensitivities. The French historian Fernand Braudel defined the Mediterranean as a "system where everything is mixed up and put back together in an original unity", requiring work for the construction of models of coexistence which I cannot set apart from differences and otherness, because the Mediterranean is

> a thousand things at once. Not a landscape but countless landscapes. Not a sea but a succession of seas. It is not a civilization, but a series of superimposed civilizations. To travel in the Mediterranean is to encounter the Roman world in Lebanon, pre-history in Sardinia, Greek cities in Sicily, the Arab presence in Spain, Turkish Islam in Yugoslavia. It is to encounter many old things which, still living, overlook the ultra-modern: next to Venice, falsely motionless, the oppressive industrial conglomeration of Mestre; beside the fisherman's boat, which is still that of Ulysses, the fishing vessel which destroys the seabed or the enormous oil tankers. It means to immerse oneself in the archaism of insular worlds and, at the same time, to be astonished by the extreme youthfulness of very ancient cities, open to all the winds of culture and profit that, since centuries, oversee and consume the sea together.[2]

Carl Schmitt described the Mediterranean as a synthesis between the earth, the reign of law, and the sea kingdom of anarchy.[3] More recently, David Abulafia believed this basin to be "the most dynamic place of interaction between different societies on the face of the planet".[4] On the occasion of the meeting of reflection and spirituality "Mediterranean, a frontier of peace", held in Bari on 23 February 2020, addressing the bishops of the Mediterranean, the Holy Father emphasised the importance of reflecting on the vocation and the future of the Mediterranean, on the transmission of the faith and the promotion of peace. Pope Francis stated that

> the Mare nostrum is the physical and spiritual locus where our civilization took shape as a result of the encounter of diverse peoples. By its very configuration, this sea forces surrounding peoples and cultures to constantly interact, to recall what they have in common, and to realize that only by living in concord can they enjoy the opportunities this region offers, thanks to its resources, its natural beauty and its varied human traditions.[5]

To best explain this idea the Pope took up the thoughts of Giorgio La Pira,[6] who defined the Mediterranean as "the great Sea of Galilee", suggesting an analogy between Jesus' time and our own. Just as Jesus lived in a context of differing cultures and beliefs, so we find ourselves in a multifaceted and multiform environment, scarred by divisions and forms of inequality which increases its instability. According to Pope Francis' reflection, it seems clear that

> amid deep fault lines and economic, religious, confessional and political conflicts, we are called to offer our witness to unity and peace. We do so prompted by our faith and membership in the Church, seeking to understand the contribution that we, as disciples of the Lord, can make to all the men and women of the Mediterranean region.[7]

Starting from these preliminary reflections we will attempt to formulate an interpretation of the situations of agreement/conflict which run through the Mediterranean and put the issue of recognition at the centre. As demonstrated by multiple analyses, at stake are the dynamics of breakdown and fragmentation of the Mediterranean area which complicate the launch of ongoing and constructive dialogues between often distant and hostile sides. The idea is that they find their origin in the lack of recognition which is expressed at a number of levels in Mediterranean societies and which obliges us to highlight the interdependence between the macro-level of the dynamics and the geo-economic and geo-political choices and the micro-level of the daily life of individuals. Focus on recognition as a multi-level process provides a perspective from which to launch processes of reconstruction, dialogue and affinity which refer back to the original identity of "mediterraneus" (literally "in the middle of the lands"), in other words, that which is between the different lands, peoples and cultures and is the mediator between them.[8]

II The challenge of recognition

Part of geopolitical thought tends to place the struggles for power and access to resources at the centre of its analyses, often tackling the cultural and religious question in terms of confrontation and the clash of civilisations.[9] This type of approach often results in an underestimation of the process of breakdown underway in specific areas of the planet, which entails an increasing internal articulation with the same cultural, religious, and social universes. In terms of the Mediterranean we note that there are no homogenous and monolithic areas around the *Mare nostrum* but there is an accentuated internal differentiation about nations, regions, cities, social groups, sectors of economic life, minorities and majorities. For example, we move from the autonomist claims of Catalonia in Spain, to the conflicts between Cyrenaica and Tripolitana in Libya, to the unstable balance of national contexts such as the situation in the Lebanon and Cyprus. Situations of conflict based on religion persist and increase and have a symbolic manifestation in the Israeli-Palestinian conflict. Then there is the question of coexistence between groups, and here we may simply think of the situations in which minorities in countries such as Turkey, Egypt and Cyprus find themselves. The "Arab spring" (albeit with mixed results) forcefully raised the issue of generational claims. The increasing difficulty of relationships between the nations of Southern and Northern Europe sees the re-emergence of a southern question about the international harmony of the continent but also the internal harmony of the individual countries (for example, the inequality between the north and south of Italy). Then we also see alliances and conflicts which revolve around the management of movements of migration and the increasing lack of alignment between the interests of the countries of departure, the areas of transit, and the countries where the migrants arrive.

It does not seem too much to maintain that this examination of the conflicts and misunderstandings which the straddles the Mediterranean area, in addition to the remnants of history, also refers back to the unsatisfied desire of peoples, nations and cultures to see their own value as the *other*[10] recognised by the stakeholders, near and far, who are the actors in this drama. In an increasingly complex and multicultural picture, the ability to exercise some recognition of others seems to atrophy, even as recognition is not a one-way and one-directional process, but an exercise of reciprocity.[11] This happens in a context marked by ambivalent drives toward de-traditionalism and then neo-traditionalism, democratisation and then authoritarianism, changes which directly impact on the lives of individuals. The future of the Mediterranean area moves from the ability to outline a tendency towards recognition of the microsocial relationships which involve people of different cultures, to the level of encounter and dialogue between States, areas and worlds which differ from both a cultural and a religious perspective. Calling to mind and paraphrasing the contribution of Axel Honneth[12] it is possible to identify three processes of recognition with which many of the increasing unsatisfied needs in the Mediterranean area can reconnect. Each indicates how the formation of the identity of individual or collective subjects is mediated by the *other* and demands a "social structure which arises in social experience".[13] The first form of recognition, which exclusively concerns the sphere of primary relationships in the daily life of Mediterranean society, refers to the presence of an affective and emotive recognition of others, essential for the construction of a stable identity. It is an aspect which places at the centre the "reasons of the heart", often sacrificed to economic interests and a strategy which overwhelms the needs of people, families and communities. The failure of foundational recognition, which happens in the everyday routine of relationships, determines the manifestation of a crisis of identity with the compromise of the elementary right to act and to initiate open and constructive social relations. A strength of Mediterranean societies is their vitality, but it is equally obvious that the tactics and strategic and functional sense in which civil societies become embroiled devalue inner lives and complicate the processes of the integration of difference.

The second form of recognition is contained in legal relationships or those of a formal nature, external to the sphere of primary relations. Here the element of intersubjectivity is generalised and so one looks for a recognition of self and the other which passes through the concept of rights, which can widen or narrow on the basis of the progress of the relationship. An acquired element is respect, while failure to recognise comes to coincide with the impossibility of exercising one's own rights. It is an element which impacts all Mediterranean societies, so that there may be a positive evolution of social and juridical norms which refer to reciprocal rights and duties, between peoples, groups, social formations and institutions. This perspective allows us to grasp the withdrawal of the legal frameworks of many Mediterranean states which limit the creative and emancipatory potential of their civil societies.

Finally, the third form of recognition refers to the social approval which derives from the appreciation by others of one's life choices and values. When these are not recognised, citizenship is denied in terms of one's way of being and ideal viewpoints, with the resultant relapse in terms of integration/lack of integration and social consensus. This is a particularly important theme where the Mediterranean risks appearing as a place of conflict between opposing extremisms or totalitarianisms; suffice simply to think of the absolutism of Eurocentrism or Islam.

This rapid reconstruction of the dynamics underlying the process of recognition demonstrates how it is constructed at various levels and how it is based on delicate balances without which the risk of crisis or conflict increases. The Mediterranean area demands a multi-level approach aimed at peace, at constructive co-existence and reciprocity, which from the geopolitical perspective reaches the everyday routine of people and vice versa. Now it is about understanding who the key actors are in whom to invest, in order to oppose the failure or distortion of recognition which generates a permanent state of tension and conflict.

III The possible leadership of civil society and intermediate subjects

The construction of new relationships between States and between supranational entities is a movement greatly emphasised by geopolitics in the perspective of going further and constructing new scenarios. However, in order to fully conceive of the Mediterranean as a space of recognition, the active contribution of not necessarily political or institutional subjects located between the macro level of national and international politics and the micro level of the daily life of individual citizens is of equal importance. In the sphere of political and economic sciences these third-party entities are usually defined as "intermediary institutional subjects or bodies".[14] They are a link joining what comes from top-down and what comes from bottom-up or goes from the centre to the margins and vice versa. In this sphere we find associations of a cultural nature and religious-inspired associations, and entities of the private social sector, municipalities and local associations, which often fulfil a dual representative function, being both key players of a territory which "absorbs" extra- and supra-local demands and spokesperson for the "local" to the central institutions. In addition, and broadening the discourse to the whole social system, we can see how this mediating function is also undertaken by other entities such as organisations, associations and groups from the economic world or civil society, which constitute groups which dialogue both with the most basic levels of society and with those which are more institutionalised and complex. It is therefore appropriate to say something about the reasons why today such intermediary entities can be key players in a *trait d'union* of the Mediterranean. Above all, this is due to the fact that they are subjects which occupy an intermediary space between the individual citizen (or the groups to which he/she belongs) and subjects of broader dimensions who increasingly prefer more formal ways of relating. The intermediary position is also between sectors as mediation is often carried out between State and Market, between public and private. In the framework of a Mediterranean area which is increasingly multicultural and complex, these intermediary subjects can undertake an important role in initiating and supporting processes of recognition. Intermediate subjects can contribute, at the invitation of Pope Francis, to making concrete the building of "institutions that can guarantee equal opportunities and enable citizens to assume their responsibility for the common good", starting precisely from the Mediterranean, and initiating a dialogue which enables encounter, the overcoming of prejudices and stereotyping, to describe and learn more about oneself and others.

IV Conclusion: a new way of thinking about the Mediterranean
The reflections contained in the preceding paragraphs show that it is not possible to approach the Mediterranean with just one vision or from points

of view which hide a presumption of absoluteness. To think about the Mediterranean means to think about difference, plurality, and otherness, and means to pick up today the challenge of recognition without which any process of welcome and integration, any peace plan or pact of solidarity, risks being slowed down or even dismissed. To focus on the roles of the different intermediary components of the societies which make up the Mediterranean, and on their capacity for inter-mediation between levels of social and political life, is not an easy path to pursue, but it is necessary for the growth of a new awareness which leads to understanding this area as a place of pluralism which does not lead to fragmentation, and a place of collaboration which does not lead to manipulation. Beyond the schematic representations and the variable intensity of relations between the States, Mediterranean societies are increasingly characterised by the common theme of difference which runs through them and which risks re-igniting (or exacerbating) excruciating conflicts. To understand the Mediterranean as space of recognition allows both the provision of a common goal and the sharing of a means to enter into the different contexts of crisis and tackle the challenges of our time. Knowing full well that if it is difficult to find the common traits of a Mediterranean culture which inevitably is plural and in continuous movement, to understand the Mediterranean as a space of recognition enables one to understand that in this historical stage Mediterranean societies are called to tackle the same challenges and internally compete with the same needs of recognition which demand the promotion of the positive intertwining between appreciation of diversity and protection of human dignity.

Translated by Patricia and Liam Kelly

Notes

1. D. John, *People of the Mediterranean: Essay in Comparative Social Anthropology*, Routledge and Kegan Paul Books, London 1977.
2. F. Braudel, *Il Mediterraneo*, Bompiani, Milan 1987, p. 12.
3. C. Schmitt, "Sovranità dello Stato e libertà dei mari", in A. Campi (eds), *L'unità del mondo e altri saggi*, Pellicani, Rome 2003, p. 148.
4. D. Abulafia, *The Great Sea: A Human History of the Mediterranean*, Allen Lane, London 2011.

5. Francis, *Meeting of reflection and spirituality "Mediterranean, a frontier of peace"* (19-23 February 2020); https://press.vatican.va/content/salastampa/it/bollettino/pubblico/2020/02/23/0119/00263.html#en

6. G. La Pira, 'Le attese della povera gente', in *Cronache sociali* 1/1950.

7. Francis, *Meeting of reflection and spirituality "Mediterranean, a frontier of peace"* (19-23 February 2020); https://press.vatican.va/content/salastampa/it/bollettino/pubblico/2020/02/23/0119/00263.html#en

8. The Mediterranean as "medius" and "medium" is also found in the names given to it by other cultures, for instance the Arabic البحر الأبيض المتوسط *al-Baḥr al-Abyaḍ al-Mutawassiṭ*, that is 'White Sea in the Middle', and Turkish *Akdeniz* 'White Sea'. In other languages there is recourse to borrowing from Latin or Neo-latin languages (e.g. the English *Mediterranean Sea*) to express the meaning of "middle sea, in the midst (of the lands)" (e.g. the German *Mittelmeer*, Hebrew *Hayam Hatikhon* (וְהַיָּם הַתִּיכוֹן), "the sea in the middle", Berber *ilel Agrakal*, 'sea between the lands', Japanese *Chichūkai* (地中海), 'sea in the middle of the lands', Albanian *deti mesdhe*, 'The sea in the middle of the lands').

9. S. Huntington, *The Clash of Civilizations and the Remaking of World Order*, Simon & Schuster, New York 1996.

10 A. Honneth, *The Struggle for Recognition: The Moral Grammar of Social Conflicts*, Polity Press, London 1996.

11. J. Habermas and C. Taylor, *Multiculturalismo. Lotte per il riconoscimento*, Feltrinelli, Milan 2001.

12. Cf. A. Honneth, *The Struggle for Recognition: The Moral Grammar of Social Conflicts*.

13. G. H. Mead, *Mind, Self, and Society: From the Standpoint of a Social Behaviorist*, University of Chicago Press, Chicago 1934.

14. Cf. A. Arrighetti and G. Seravalli, *Istituzioni intermedie e sviluppo locale*, Donzelli, Rome 1999.

Theology *from* the Mediterranean

GIUSEPPINA DE SIMONE

What does doing theology in the Mediterranean mean and what has the Mediterranean got to say about the understanding of the faith? Beyond the supposed rigidity of the borders to be defended at all costs, the Mediterranean is the 'sea that is also a crossroads', which speaks of cultural identities made by exchanges and contaminations: plural and multiple landscapes, cultures, traditions, and yet undoubtedly 'one'. A theology from the Mediterranean is a theology capable of discerning the signs of the Kingdom of God in the folds of history and understanding prophetically the signs of the anti-Kingdom that disfigure the soul and human history; a 'performative interpretation' which encourages the assumption of responsibility; a theology of dialogue and possible fraternity, beyond borders and with the capacity to inhabit them.

Introduction

What does it mean to do theology in the Mediterranean?

In the reflection I offer I will start from the Mediterranean and the importance to it of borders, so as next to clarify why and how theology must be concerned about the Mediterranean, in order finally to look at what the Mediterranean has to say to theology. The hinterland to this reflection is the work we have been doing for a number of years in Naples with the two-year specialisation in Fundamental Theology in the San Luigi Section of the Pontifical Theological Faculty of Southern Italy.

I A question of borders: between history and narration

If we sought to suggest an image of the Mediterranean, to be able to think about it in its concrete reality, we would immediately run into the question of borders.

The Mediterranean is a question of borders.[1] The borders are not drawn by the seas or mountains, but by the relationships built by history between peoples and the places they inhabit. The borders are history and have the fluidity of history and the sign of change. What is more, borders are the narrative of history, a representation of relationships of strength which are established in a space that is itself fluid, a space of passages, of confrontations, and of conflicts, but still of relationships, whether they are taken up or denied.

More than ever in the Mediterranean, borders elude too clear a definition and evade any pretence of steadiness. The drama of migrations and the reactions they cause – from the common clichés straddled by politics, to the secret but real attitude which sometimes underlies interventions of a charitable nature – fractures an image of the Mediterranean constructed by the categories of inside-out, north-south, civilisation-underdevelopment, recalling ancient events and bringing to the fore spaces and cultures which are part of the Mediterranean, but which some would like to think of as guests, gracefully welcomed or poorly tolerated, but still requiring admission.[2]

In reality the sea is the space of relationships and passages par excellence.[3] Now this sea too states what is at stake in this corner of the earth which has returned to being dramatically central for the battles fought in it. It is here that the possibility of life or death is gambled with death, the possibility of recognition or rejection of the other, the possibility of memory or the possibility of giving life to new narratives.

The fundamental question is precisely one of narrative. It is also a hermeneutical question. The narrative is born from a thought which runs through events and reads them, still starting from a theoretical frame of reference, within a tradition and a shared memory which is itself built through interpretation, in a hermeneutical circle of which we must always be aware.

A sterile interpretation or one absolutely consistent with the facts is never given. Rather, it is putting oneself in front of them, being involved in them, which provides the possibility of developing an understanding of them.

So then, to recover the interpretative dimension of the image of the Mediterranean, to rediscover the responsibility of discernment, looking at the borders and knowing how to inhabit them with the intelligence of history and a profound sense of the human, become priority tasks. New narratives are possible, in the principle of fraternity and dialogue, but only if we know how to develop an adequate awareness of what is at stake and what is underlying the readings in the field.

II What has this got to do with theology?
At this point one might ask what has this got to do with theology? The Introduction to *Veritatis Gaudium* springs to mind: ecclesiastical studies 'constitute a sort of providential cultural laboratory in which the Church carries out the performative interpretation of the reality brought about by the Christ event'.[4] This is not an idea, but the person of Jesus Christ in whom the whole of history, and our humanity itself, was assumed and brought to fulfilment. He is the light in whom we discover the meaning of what we experience. And it is not a light which is behind us, in a distant past, something which happened once and for all, to which all events can be traced back in a regressive moment, nor even a light which is permanently before us, in a real but very distant *eschaton*, to strive towards knowing the whole difference which exists between fulfilment and expectation, between happening and the end of time, between the temporary and the eternal. The light of Christ, the light which is Christ, enlightens from within the event of history so that it is not extraneous to it. The logic of the incarnation is not a logic of a practical nature, but a beginning of understanding of the reality which recognises in it the operative presence of the Lord Jesus and of his Pasch. To proclaim the Gospel is not remembering the past, but helping to read the present, to glimpse in it the action of God who precedes and guides without ever forcing or pre-determining human action.

Therefore theology cannot be built in the laboratory, cannot be abstract knowledge satisfied with the formal perfection of its reasoning, preoccupied solely with the technical rigour of the categories used and by the logical coherence of its reason. Theology is built on the street, among the people, in the folds of experience. It requires competence and rigour, like every science; but it must become 'wise', because more than anything else what nourishes it is that ability to listen which is contemplation.

The Church Fathers and the great theologians of every age certainly understood this, knowing how to introduce the rigour of thought in a living relationship to the concrete nature of common experience.

III History as "theological locus": theology in context

At a theological level, too, there is no lack of references for setting the theme of the value of the experience which human beings build in history for a more profound understanding of the Gospel.

Since it is true that the Gospel enlightens history, it is also true that history is the 'theological locus' and that its event is not a mere succession of events, but the warp and weft of meaning within which the Gospel continues to speak out, and from which, despite uncertainties, sinuosity and errors, we are given to understand God's salvific plan ever more. To speak of history as 'theological locus' does not in fact mean simply to recognise that God revealed himself in history, but to enhance the profound awareness that God continues to speak through history and that therefore we can speak of God by recounting the history we experience, perceiving its deepest direction of meaning and learning to narrate it. And we can speak to God by giving shape to history, taking on responsibility for it, because the narrative passes through our lives, the relationships we know how to create, the balances to which we give life in the relationship with things and with the world, the environment we design around us.

It is in this sense that we can speak of 'contextual' theology, recognising that theology cannot be done everywhere in the same way,[5] but that theology must breathe the air of the place in which it is constructed, and not in a sense merely applicable to local translation, but one of inspiration, of inner incentive and dominant tone, since the gospel has the colours of the peoples and the different and plural tones of the cultures.

IV Towards a theology in the context of the Mediterranean

Pope Francis has often returned to the theme of theology in context, beginning with his message to the theologians of Argentina.[6] He spoke about it particularly in Naples, at the conference which took place on 21 June 2019 promoted by the San Luigi Section of the PFTIM. For some years here in Naples we have been asking what it means to do theology in the Mediterranean and from this wide-ranging discussion arose the new course of Specialisation in Fundamental Theology, *Theology of religious experience in the Mediteranean context.*

The lesson given by Pope Francis at that conference affirmed and clarified the insights which guided us, tracing the coordinates of a theology in the context of the Mediterranean which has a lot to say to theology as such. The Mediterranean, as the Pope often emphasises, is 'the sea that is also a crossroads'.[7] Where the borders do not hold, where starting from listening to the roots and to the present, there is a need for 'renewed and shared narratives... in which it is possible to see oneself in a constructive, peaceful and hope-generating way'.[8]

Theology can contribute to creating these narratives, due to its profoundly ecclesial character, because it is not a discourse of specialists but the understanding of the faith of the Church and the Church is a Church of people. If there is a specific expertise belonging to it, it is that of the masses, of being mixed in with the life of the ordinary people. And it is from this perspective, from the side of the little ones, especially the poor, from the point of view which is given by the lived experience of the ordinary people, that the Church, and with it theology, can speak about the Mediterranean. Without chasing sweetened visions and far from artificial ideological contrasts between the people and the elite the fact remains that 'the reality is superior to the idea' and that the life of the ordinary people, when it is not warped by those who exploit fear and uncertainty, says quite something else of the determined defence of identity borders. This is also the case because the identity of the people is made up of relations and connections which extend in time, which summarise what comes from exchanges, encounters, and even conflicts. What purity of culture or of tradition can be claimed in the history of humanity if not the mad ideological constructions of totalitarianisms with their destructive violence? Suffice to wander the streets of our cities, to contemplate their architecture and the symbolic language of the art, to taste the flavours and recall the customs and traditions, to understand the layers and the productive contamination lie at the origin of that identity that one would like to claim as "pure".

So what can it mean to do theology in the Mediterranean or how must a theology which is built as understanding of the faith in this specific context be shaped? Pope Francis stated it very clearly.

It must be a *theology in dialogue* capable of reading in reality theological connections and references; of 'discerning the signs of the Kingdom of God in history and [able] to understand prophetically the signs of the anti-Kingdom that disfigure the soul and human history' and of grasping what efforts the Spirit is arousing here and now;[9] capable above all of doing this in dialogue with the different knowledges, whose contribution it welcomes in a trans-disciplinarity manner which becomes style and method of research.

A theology of listening which, like "spiritual ethnographers", knows how to push forward to 'where paradigms, ways of feeling, symbols, and representations of individuals and of peoples are formed',[10] so as to be able to dialogue in depth.

A theology of compassion which allows itself to be "touched" by people's lives and by 'the enormous injustices suffered by so many poor people who live on the shores of this "common sea"'.[11]

A theology which has *the courage of creativity* and knows how to try new paths leaving room for the novelties of the Spirit.

A theology of the people of God working towards 'a "theological Pentecost", which allows the women and men of our time to hear "in their own native language" a Christian message that responds to their search for meaning and for a full life'.[12]

V The Mediterranean as "theological locus"
But if it makes no difference to do theology in different contexts, neither does how much that context has to say to understanding of the faith. And it is this which drives us to speak about the Mediterranean as "theological locus".

The Mediterranean implies a generative space in which began the great civilisations which marked the world's history began, as did the three great monotheistic faiths which have played such a role in the affairs of the whole of humanity. It is the space in which the Gospel was first transmitted, through the journeys which crossed it, revolutionising the vision of humanity and the relationships which define humanity. But the Mediterranean has been, and is, a space of conflicts, of abuses of power and violence carried out in the name of God. It is the cradle of humanism and of the Arab civilisation in its greatest intellectual and artistic flowering, but it is also the space where the drama takes place of oppressed lives trampled on, rights ignored, deaths occurring through general indifference, the repeated denial of the other. From cradle to tomb, the Mediterranean invites reflection on the interweaving of life and death, on the fragility of the border between these two apparently opposed possibilities, on the value of recognition and welcome because it is life. And once again it is here, in rejection or welcome, that the negation or generation of the human is at stake, because the question of migrants is not just the question of desperate people being allowed to land on the coasts of the richest countries or to cross boundaries in search of a better life. It is also the question of wars and famines, of droughts and corruption which torment the countries from which they have come, the fruit of politics gone wrong, of international power games, of external economic interests, repeated extortion and the desire to dominate unscrupulously. The migration of peoples "forced to flee" reminds us of what forces them and what we do not want to see: they revealing the imbalances and injustices of which we must rather become aware in order to try and build a more human world. So, it is the signs of the anti-Kingdom which theology can denounce in the indifference and hostility of those who close the door, defend borders or build walls, in the Mediterranean as elsewhere.

Theology has much to learn from a deeper knowledge of the Mediterranean's conflicts and the reasons for them, as well as from the intertwining of the Mediterranean geopolitics with all its multiple and complex implications, so as not to risk limiting itself to a naïve explanation of principles, and to form instead a more mature capacity for discernment and judgement and more informed assumption of responsibility. This is what we are seeking to do through our Specialisation, also making room for courses in geopolitics and theological courses of peace and promotion of justice.

But the Mediterranean also recounts tales of fruitful contamination between cultures, and it is the narrative of art and forms of daily life; it is the narrative of popular religiosity in its centuries-old stratification and in the needs which run through it. There is a grammar of human experience in which borders are more porous than ever, and the mutual exchanges and convergences are far more than we can imagine, where the affinities of identity fade and we recognise each other. For this, an important space in our journey of studies is reserved for the language of art, in particular through courses with the School of Art and theology; and the study of popular religiosity, keeping together the experience of a direct contact with the territory and theoretical detailed study.[13]

It is on this side of everyday life and the basic forms of the cultures in their mutual appeal, that one captures the most typical feature of the Mediterranean, its being profoundly marked by diversity, characterised by a variety of landscapes, of cultures, of traditions, and yet being undoubtedly "one". Because beyond the borders and maps, beyond the walls and the hardening identities, there is a common air in the Mediterranean. It is breathed above all living in its cities: Naples, Palermo, Jerusalem, and others, and in encounter with those who never tire of continuing to weave threads of encounter in prayer, in ecumenical and inter-religious dialogue, in support for the poorest to build with them a better world, in academic research: testimonies which have helped us to understand this Mediterranean style and to breathe its beauty in our itinerant courses and in the encounters conceived as an integral part of our formative proposal.[14]

Unity in diversity is the great challenge experienced by the Mediterranean and it is the most proper indicator of the communion and fraternity we are called to build as the whole of humanity. Such unity is given at the root and is before us as goal, terminus of the stretching out of history of human beings and of the heart's desire as harmony of diversity. In the path of history, this harmony, which the Spirit never ceases to arouse, is shaped like a polyhedron in which differences appear not in a symphony which eliminates the strain of differences, but in convergences of the multiple facets, which do not hide the toughness of the encounter, while demonstrating its possibility and profound beauty. So it is in the Mediterranean. So in our itinerary of studies we make room for knowledge of the religious traditions, of the languages and cultures which inhabit the Mediterranean through the contribution of those who have direct knowledge of them through belonging to them. The presence in our faculty of professors of scholars from countries with a Muslim tradition or from Israel, the study of Arabic and Semitic cultures, discussion with the Orthodox tradition, has given us the possibility of probing these different cultural worlds, learning to know them from within, in what is proper to them, but also in the transformations and demands they are experiencing today.

A theology *from* is a theology of fraternity: sought, awaited, discovered as gift among the folds of history and as desire in the heart of human beings, recognised as a challenge, but also as the implicit figure of a Mediterranean which is irreducibly plural and together one. It is a theology which never tires of proclaiming the Kingdom of God as the fulfilment of human history and never tires of demanding an active and responsible commitment for its construction in the passage of time. Because theology is not everything, but it can motivate the commitment and assumption of responsibility if it allows itself to be challenged by experience, to be moved by the concreteness of the experience we are in with the richness of our faith, if it accepts being, according to the logic of the incarnation, within a context, providing a "performative interpretation" of it. A cultural laboratory, a space of new and fruitful narrative beyond the boundaries and with the capacity to inhabit them.

Translated by Patricia and Liam Kelly

Notes

1. See the interesting study by Iain Chambers and Marta Cariello, *La questione mediterranea*, Mondadori, Città di Castello (PG) 2019.
2. *Cf. ibid.*, 28-41; 44-51; Iain Chambers, *Sulla soglia del mondo.L'altrove dell'Occidente*, Meltemi, Rome 2003.
3. *Cf.* Id., *Le molte voci del Mediterraneo*, Raffaello Cortina, Milan 2007, 5-7.
4. Francis, Apostolic Constitution *Veritatis Gaudium* on Ecclesiastical Universities and Faculties, *Foreword* n.3.
5. See Hans Waldenfels, *Teologia fondamentale nel contesto contemporaneo*, 2nd edn, San Paolo, Cinisello Balsamo 1996. On the contextual nature of theology *cf* also Giuseppe Lorizio, *Le frontiere dell'amore. Saggi di teologia fondamentale,* Lateran University Press, Città del Vaticano 2009; Vincenzo Di Pilato, *Discepoli della Via.* Questioni e prospettive sul metodo della teologia, Città Nuova, Rome 2019.
6. *Cf* Letter to the Grand Chancellor of the Pontificia Universidad Catholica Argentina on the centenary of the Faculty of Theology, 3 March 2015.
7. Francis, *Theology after* Veritatis Gaudium *in the context of the Mediterranean*, Naples 21 June 2019, in Secondo Bongiovanni - Sergio Tanzarella (eds.), *Con tutti i naufraghi della storia*, Il pozzo di Giacobbe, Trapani 2019, 226.
8. *Ibid.*
9. *Ibid.*, 222-223.
10. *Ibid.*
11. *Ibid.*, 227.
12. *Ibid.*, 230.

13. Some texts have already arisen from this work: Emilio Salvatore and Carmelo Torcivia, *Quando a credere è il popolo. Tensioni e ricomposizioni di un'esperienza religiosa*, Il pozzo di Giacobbe, Trapani 2019; Giuseppina De Simone (ed.), *La devozione popolare tra Arte e Teologia*, Quaderni della Scuola di Alta Formazione di Arte e Teologia -Nuova Serie 2020; Giorgio Agnisola, *Arte e dialogo nel Mediterraneo,* Il pozzo di Giacobbe, Trapani 2020; and more generally the volumes published in the "Sponde" series with Il pozzo di Giacobbe publishers.

14. See the Specialisation's website: www.specializzazioneteologiafondamentalepftim.it

Part Three: Epilogue

Art Borders Beyond Borders

CRISPINO VALENZIANO

I

The word – BORDER – has given me and continues to give much food for thought, raising in many eloquent theories and intriguing ideas. Here, in front of the wonderful Pentecost mosaic, iconologically and iconographically, a *unicum* in the universe of Christian art, a *hapax* that we will encounter in the Palatine Chapel of Roger II in Palermo.

I received confirmation of my hermeneutics from M. Crociata, former professor of Fundamental Theology in the Theological Faculty of Sicily, then Secretary General of the Italian Episcopal Conference, now Bishop of Latina and related dioceses, and Vice-President of the Commission of Bishops in the European Union:

Let's cross the theme of the "border". It is interesting to observe what C. Yannaras writes about it: "Facing heresies, the Church has reacted by fixing the boundaries of the truth, that is, by outlining its own lived experience. It is very significant that the first designation given to what we now call dogma was *horos*, 'border', frontier of truth (in Latin, *terminus*)" (*La fede nell'esperienza ecclesiale. Introduzione alla teologia ortodossa*, Queriniana, Brescia 1983, 30). But K. Rahner considers the theme from a different perspective: "The dogmatic formula is a 'term', a result in which everything also depends on the fact that the term is a 'beginning'. From the essence of human knowledge of truth and from the nature of divine truth it results that a single truth is a starting point and not a conclusion" (*Saggi di cristologia e di mariologia*, Paoline, Roma 1967, 3s.). […] We can draw the conclusion that "border" embraces the dual value of limit and horizon. It is not an opposing or alternative duplicity, since it suggests that believing is not a path in which to worry about going astray , so to speak, but from where to proceed forward, opening up to the wide horizon of the boundless horizon of faith.[1]

The focus of M. Crociata therefore leads us to realize that "border" is "frontier", *terminus*, as "mountain" (see *horos* in Mt 28,16; Mc 6,46; Lk 6,12; 21,37; 22,39, Joh 6,3.15), and that "the end" is a beginning rather than a conclusion. Moreover, the noun *horos* "border" is limit and end and the verb *horizo* means to determine, delimit and establish (see *horizo* in Act 2,32; 10,42; 11,29; 17,26.31; Rom 1,4; Heb 4,7). It also means "to look/see ahead", "to look/see far away": *prospectus*. Exactly, "horizon".

It is a complex reality on which to reflect broadly and deeply! And in this regard, I immediately note that my very short paper can refer only to one graphical reproduction; it cannot relate the colour of the mosaics and can only hint at traces of reflection.

II

I asked the architect Tania Culotta, daughter of P. Culotta who was dean of the Faculty of Architecture at the University of Palermo and Academic of San Luca, to draw me three diagrams with precise designations:

1. – of the architectural square that is and that was the oriental-syriac cultic ensemble of "Santa Maria dell'Ammiraglio";

2. – of the corresponding box that, with its longitudinal intercolumn attached as an extension to the rectangular hall, forms the *bema* (from *baino*, going up), the "trend"/the "occidental-roman" rialto towards the Altar, of the Chapel "San Pietro *in Palatio*" – the Palatine Chapel of Roger II, the Norman first king of Sicily;

3. – of the side wall in the *diakonicon*, approaching (under the wonderful vault with Pentecost *hapax*) the Mysteries of Christ "Light-Life" and focuses on the revelatory selection of the Only-Begotten of God "Son of Man" all around his Transfiguration on the "mountain".

This refers "beyond" any points of reference. But I think it is useful, and indeed necessary, to place oneself above the visual awareness of the "beyond" that we are looking for. Therefore, for a motivated and motivating awareness, I add to the three architectural schemes the photo of the vault that curves on the Pentecost.

Because of the luminescence of "John" in the Fourth Gospel, and in the First Letter addressed to the communities of Asia wounded by the first ecclesial lacerations of their faith, it is important to lift this up in our discourse. Here is the stimulating sillogism from the "defending" Paraclete, in the Letter to the "consoling" Paraclete, in the Gospel:

"My little children, [...] we have the Paraclete, *parakleton*, Jesus Christ the righteous." (1 John 2,1)
"And I will pray the Father, and he will give you another Paraclete, *allon parakleton*, to be with you for ever." (John 14,16)
"But the Paraclete, the Holy Spirit, *ho de Parakletos to pneuma to hagion*, whom the Father will send in my name, he will teach you all things, and bring to your remembrance all that I have said to you." (John 14,26)
"But when the Paraclete comes, *otan de elthe ho parakletos*, whom I shall send to you from the Father, even the Spirit of truth, who proceeds from the Father, he will bear witness to me." (John 15,26)
"If I do not go away, the Paraclete will not come to you *ouk eleusehai pros ymas*." (John 16,7).

The waters in the sea collect and condense more and better than the mountains on earth. In the Mediterranean, Christianity has experienced this phenomenon since its origins for the archaic Churches of the "five patriarchates" have proliferated here: from the Mother Church of Jerusalem to the venerable Churches of Antioch, Rome, Byzantium, and Alexandria, that regardless of their even at times adverse vicissitudes have germinated the Church in the whole inhabited world.

It is necessary to *visit*, "inspect by, looking for", the Mediterranean, where different lands of different "continents" overlook each other. And there even isolated lands – "islands" – float in search of authenticity for themselves and others. According to C.M. Martini, «to be authentic means to be *authos*, oneself, fully oneself; while we are half hidden and what we say is not the fullness of our ego».[2]

Small digression? The "pandemic" of our times – if I may say so: the "pandemonium" of our days – in my opinion does not resolve itself by assuming a "new Christianity".

> When you hear that, among the Churches, one has fallen to the bottom, another is at the mercy of the waves, one has suffered irreparable damage, the other has a wolf in place of a shepherd and another a pirate in place of a helmsman, and yet another a murderer in place of a doctor, all right, grieved, because similar evils are not bearable without suffering all the torment. But grieve with measure, *metron*, in your pain... Because to yearn and fall into depression [...] for the mistakes of others is useless exasperation [...]; worse: it's a diabolical and lethal situation.[3]

If we aim to dream, having closed the doors providentially opened by the Second Vatican Council "borders" – "measures" – more and better suited to us, it will be more and better profitable to daydream of a "brand new Catholicism".

III In the island of Sicily; in Palermo, around the middle of the XII century

3.1 Santa Maria dell'Ammiraglio and Cappella Palatina

Their "Byzantine" characteristic is marked by the various types of proximity to the synchronous mosaics in the south matroneum of St. Sophia in Constantinople. However this leads us to other assemblages. The two architectures, similarly mosaicized by technique, do not deceive us. For in the church of the Admiral and in the church of the King, the graphically unified and unifying art conveys the identity of each one's rite and celebration.[4] Here I would just like to remind us that both domes in our two images bear the Eucharistic Anaphora of the Celebration according to each of the two Rites. Rite and Celebration in both cases are as distant as the Syrian "cultic culture" in Antioch from the Byzantine "cultic culture" of Constantinople. It is precisely the "culture" that points to the "beyond", the boundaries. Because Culture and Cult, from *colere*, are both "cultivations".

fig. 1: Church S. Maria dell'Ammiraglio, called "La Martorana": scheme of the mosaics;

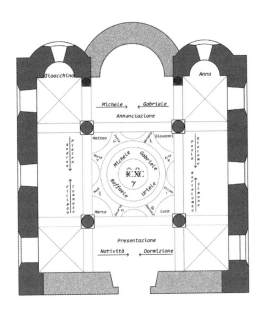

fig. 2: Church S. Pietro in Palatio, called "Cappella Palatina": scheme of
the mosaics on the *bema*

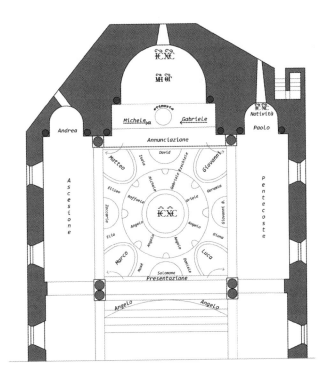

3.2 The Side Wall of the Diakonicon and the Vault of Pentecost

fig. 3: Church of S. Pietro in Palatio, called "Cappella Palatina": scheme of the mosaics of the *diakonikon*

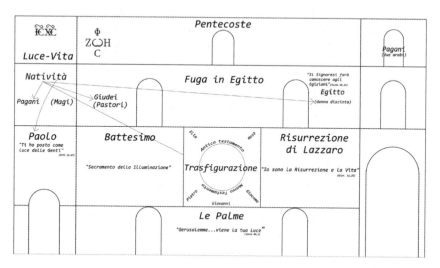

The theme of Christ Jesus Light/Life takes place starting from his Nativity. The relative mosaic inscription sings the Theotokos, Parent of the Son of God who is born from her Son of Man among us:

Stella parit Solem	The star generates the Sun
Rosa Florem	the rose the Flower
Forma decorem	the Form a graceful appearance».

It is amazing that, as lesser star, she generates the greater star; that the flower is generated from the rose. The Flower stands for eminence from rose par excellence. It is astounding that the most formidable Woman generates the Beauty exceeding all the beauties.

It is for this reason that the icon of the beauty of the Pantocrator is harmoniously counterpointed with the narrability of the event at which the new Adam is born among us and takes the "form" of the ancient Adam.

From his Birth he gathers together the People of Israel – representing them with the shepherds and the other People of the World represented by the Magi –, the theme *ΦΩΣ/ΖΩΗ* advances until his entrance into Jerusalem for the "Passion", until his Death and Resurrection.

Representations of the theme: the Flight into Egypt, in the manner of all refugees of every time and place to his baptism which he will confer on him the Holy Spirit; to the resurrection of Lazarus in the manner of all who believe in him. And the Apostle Paul, called from among the People of Israel and placed to shed light on the other People.

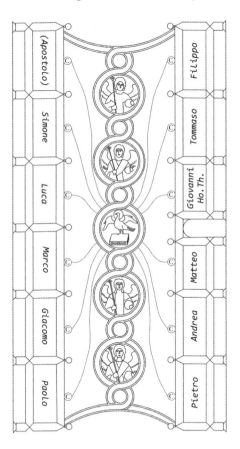

fig. 4: Church of S. Pietro in Palatio, called "Cappella Palatina": south transept vault

Type: the Transfiguration in the manner of the three, Peter James John, with the New Alliance, or of the two, Moses and Elijah, with the Old Law.

> Elijah was a man with a nature like ours (James 5,17); (The winners) sing the song of Moses, the servant of God: "For You alone are holy. For all nations shall come before You» (Rev 15,3-4). And we heard this voice (of God) which came from heaven when we were with Him on the holy mountain, *syn auto ontes en to horei haghio* (2 Pt 1,18); Jesus took Peter, James, [...] and led them up on a high mountain (Mt 17,1); Jesus took Peter, James, and John, and led them up on a high mountain (Mk 9,2); He took Peter, John, and James and went up on the mountain (Lk 9,28).

The two are the witnesses to the ancient Prophecy and the ancient Law; but the three are the *horos*, the high mountain, the holy mountain of the border "beyond"...

The mysterious intensity of the historical dynamics is all mosaicized with the descent of the Holy Spirit. Once again a poetic theme expresses the astonishment running all around the icons of Pentecost:

Fit sonus e coelis	A rumble comes from the sky
et iuxta scripta Johelis	and according to which is written in Joel
imbuit afflatus	the wind descends
sonat vehementis flatus	vehemently renews the Blow
pectora mundorum	the heart of the already pure
succendens discipulorum	disciples by lighting
ut Vitae Verbum	so that the Word of Life
per eos terat superbum	for them through annihilate the superb.

It is astonishing that Peter the Apostle in this way, through the Holy Spirit who enkindles his already pure heart, proclaims fulfilled what is written in Joel the prophet: I will pour out of my Spirit upon all flesh: and your sons and your daughters shall prophesy [...]. I will pour out in those days of my Spirit; and they shall prophesy (Acts 2,16-18/Joel 3,1-2). And it is astonishing that in this way, by the proclamation of the prophets and the apostles in the Holy Spirit vehemently blowing, the Word of Life annihilates all diabolical, "separating" pride.

The Pentecost icon (Acts 2,1-4), unique of its kind, has no equal representation, let's repeat it. An elegant interweaving of roundels knotted in chain and surrounded with finesse runs through the vault of the entire *diakonicon* invading it completely. In the central round a bright dove in a halo stands alone, in the previous two and in the following two we find the four archangels deacons, Michele Gabriele Raffaele Uriele, dressed in dalmatic and stole, posed for liturgical service with Eucharistic *ripidion* and *kerameus*. From the centre twelve tongues of fire radiate, twelve very long flame-red rivers that host twelve doves of similar brightness, but not similarly nimbates that are directed to the apostles in two side choirs – among the twelve, albeit different, we number Paul who was filled with the Holy Spirit in Damascus, not in Jerusalem (Acts 9:17-18) and Luke the hagiographer of the iconological text for iconographic elaboration. On the short wall opposite the Pantocrator two of the Mediterranean ecumene listed in the Lucanian text (Acts 2,9-11) are represented.

It is an *hapax* icon; but it is sapid of the liturgical, ritualistic, celebratory mystagogy of Pentecost: We pray to you, God Pantocrator, give us that the splendour of your Brightness may shine upon us and the Light of your Light may confirm with the Brightness of your Holy Spirit the hearts of those who are reborn by virtue of your Grace» (Prayer, currently second, in the Eucharistic liturgy of the vigil of Pentecost). Icon of the Church of God One-Trine "friend of men", in the ecclesial hall of Christ God-Man Risen Lord.

IV

I write today September 27, 2020. Sunday XXVI of the Liturgical Time not specifically named during the year. The collected prayer of the Assembly gathered for the celebration of the Eucharist is addressed, surprisingly, to God Panto/Chrator.

The Greek *Panta/Krator* is translated in Latin as *Omnia/Potens*, "in all and for all Powerful", using a translation that to me seems "weak", reductive of the "strong" starting language. But the mysterious qualification of the initial vocative qualification is as unexpected as really moving: *Deus qui*

Omni/Potentiam tuam… maxime miserando manifestas… O God who summarily reveals your being Panta/Krator demonstrating your Mercy…. In my opinion, the icon of our Panto/Creator "Light-Life"… is beautifully "tuned". In fact, the antiphon of entrance to the same Eucharistic celebration, instead of a Psalm in the most usual way, exclaims in the least rehearsed way the verses of a Song that we know to be "martyrial": Do with us according to the excess of your Mercy, give Glory Lord to your Name! (Song of Azariah in the burning furnace, Daniel 3,42-43).

Notes

1. Mariano Crociata, "Il Simbolo, «confine» della educazione alla Fede?", in AA.VV., *Ridire il Credo oggi*, EDB, Bologna 2015, 33-42; here 40-41.
2. Carlo Maria Martini, *Uomini di riconciliazione e di pace*, Borla, Roma 1984, 20.
3. John Chrysostom, *Letter to Olimpia* 8, 1, d-e.
4. B. Rocco meticulously narrated them in "*Ho Theologos*. Cultura Cristiana di Sicilia", n.2-3/1974, pp. 194-219, for the first, e n. 11-12/1976, pp. 122-174, for the second. Notes

Part Five: Theological Forum

Written by Clowns…
Supervised by Monkeys:[1]
A Critique of the Covid-19 Narrative

KRISTOF K. P. VANHOUTTE

The Covid-19 pandemic has changed the world how we know it (at least for now). The question is, was this change justified? In this provocation, I will list three critiques to the narrative (the newly invented narrative) with and through which we have been making sense of the events of this pandemic as they have been unfolding. The three main groups of authors of this new narrative: politicians, medical experts, and the mass media professionals, are being put in front of some basic critique. This provocation concludes with the discouraging awareness that accountability will not be part of this narrative.

"What one cannot speak about we must pass over in silence" is the metaphysical, if not purely mystical, statement with which Ludwig Wittgenstein ends his *Tractatus Logico-Philosophicus*. Immanentizing and even contextualizing this assertion, I will pass over in silence the medical sphere. I am no medical doctor and so I will not utter any medical claim. Furthermore, and this needs to be clear from the beginning: I will not question the "fact" of the epidemic or pandemic as the Italian philosopher Giorgio Agamben has done. Or, more precisely, I will not deny the existence of a deadly virus that has been, first, labeled as an epidemic, and, later, as a pandemic.[2]

I am aware that there are medical implications connected to my comments. They, however, do not belong to my competencies. Although this might be considered as problematic (I am open to critique), the conditional nature of this statement is certainly more laudable than the blind ignorance regarding the implications of the statements made by the various "experts" on the spheres beyond their competence.

*

That one will not touch upon medical issues when talking about an epi/pandemic should, however, not alarm. As the epidemiologist Philip Alcabes wrote in his *Dread: How Fear and Fantasy Have Fueled Epidemics from the Black Death to Avian Flu,*[3] there are three diverse and equally important categories involved in the understanding and dealing with an epi/pandemic. True, while these categories are profoundly and intricately related, they play themselves out on different fields.

1. The physical and biological event of the disease
2. The social implications (the social crisis) caused by the biological event
3. The narration of the epi/pandemic (the storyline of the unfolding of the events that allows people to make sense of what happens/happened)

In what follows, I will only confront the third aspect.

The reason most countries (especially those that went for a system of complete lockdown) only took into consideration the physical/biological category, ignoring the other two, is the question that needs an answer. I believe the homicidal combination of fear-guilt-incompetence (in whatever order one likes) is closer to the truth than any other reason offered.[4]

*

For reasons that are still unclear (many governments are keeping fundamental documents secret), and that will need to be thoroughly examined in the future, the moment this virus started spreading, world leaders seemed to unanimously decide that we were confronted with something completely new. This implied that the narrative with and through which we were going to make sense of the events as they unfolded had to be written from scratch. And that resulting narrative has been in the best tradition of H. P. Lovecraft.

There doesn't seem to be any good reason for the decision regarding the absolute newness of this virus. It was almost immediately clear with which enemy we were dealing, and it wasn't even our first encounter with this particular type of virus.

*

For reasons related to word limits, I will only list three critiques to the invented narrative. These critical facets are, however, particularly poignant as they cover the three groups of principal authors of this disastrous narrative.

*

1. The first haunting character in the COVID-19 pandemic narrative is the continuous dismantling of trust. Trust and distrust (and its interactions) are both constituent parts of our democracies. There are even 'institutionalized' forms of distrust, and these are fundamental to and essential in letting our democracies function. However, the ordinary play between trust and distrust has been put in checkmate by a peculiar type of distrust that has come to the fore in this crisis. While distrust is an acceptable, even necessary, bottoms-up attitude, the current explicit top-down distrust of entire populations by their political leaders is not.[5] This distrust has gone so far that even the trust in the representatives of the population has been given up. Parliamentary democracy has been shelved to handle this crisis.

The various states of exception that have been declared all over the world are not just extremely worrying repetitions of the Third Reich. They are a democratically unprecedented and unjustified dismantling of the concept of trust in the socio-political field.

*

2. Not only has the COVID-19 pandemic led to a pandemic of misanthropy, what used to be regarded as our most distinguished feature – our reason – has also been downgraded and deemed untrustworthy. No effort has been made to try and explain to the people what was (thought was) happening. The earliest reactions of derision by both political leaders and medical experts made immediate way for pure panic. At no time was 'informing rationally' the chosen option.

The by now mainstream (albeit particularly destructive) conviction that (moral) panic is not necessarily bad but could even be helpful in increasing awareness, was the uniquely chosen means by which political and medical leaders communicated. However, as Frank Furedi has demonstrated so well, this reliance upon panic as a means to raise awareness and receive a hearing, even a following, is a definite indication of a loss in faith in the reasoned argument.[6]

It is in this context that one has to place the mass media's devastating role in this pandemic narrative. If panic has been used and abused in these past months, then it was in almost all the forms of communication that have been, and still are, thrown at us daily, completely forfeiting the use of argumentation and reasoning.

*

3. A third protagonist in this horror story is the sickening reliance on numerology and futurology.

On the one hand, we see a remarkable trust in a series of bare numbers. For as much as these naked numbers say nothing on their own, only one possible reading is proclaimed and allowed by the bureaucrats. And in this contemporary return of a medieval inquisition, where arbitrary orthodoxy needs to be defended by all means, it is consistently the more dystopian reading of these numbers that has the upper hand.[7]

On the other hand, there is a similarly remarkable blind trust in models and calculations about the future. Statements, proclamations and legally binding decisions are constantly being made based on nothing more than an academic form of fortune-telling. The exquisitely pedagogical saying that "all models are wrong, but they allow us to ask good questions" has been overturned into the mind numbing "all models are right, so let's stop asking questions."

It is in this context that the role of the various court virologists and epidemiologists should be situated and harshly denounced (the fact that these scientists were chosen to lead our combat against this virus should make us understand that locking down was the only option that was ever considered [massively and quickly investing in public health, for example, was never an option[8]]). Science has been downgraded by these starstruck (orgiastically twittering) wizards into nothing more than thumb-sucking, hat-throwing arbitrariness. Politicians have recently, and unfortunately, also discovered how they can use this new type of 'banana-science' in favor of their geopolitical games.

*

Many more directly or indirectly related problematics regarding the current COVID-19 pandemic narrative could and should be covered. I didn't refer to the inconsistency of and in public policy, or the blatant incoherencies in both national and international politics. Mentioning the constant presence of obvious (or less evident) lies, has by now become obsolete. Furthermore, the irrational fear that has been installed in many previously rational thinking people and the growing rate of mental health problems caused by this insane narrative, will have innumerable backlashes for decades to come. And what about the scandalous and utterly shocking disdain demonstrated towards schooling and educating?

*

But let me conclude by referring to a single word: accountability. Will there be any accountability for the authors of this devilish narrative? Will the politicians, virologists and other medical "experts", and the journalists who have helped create this destructive account, ever be required to take responsibility for their actions?

I'm probably too cynical to even consider responding to that question.

Notes

1. This is a slightly altered phrase from the one made by a pilot regarding the creation of the disaster-struck Boeing 737 Max airplane. The original phrase was "*designed* by clowns, supervised by monkeys". As I will focus on narratives, the verb 'design' did not fit, so I changed it with 'write'. I leave it up to the various leaders involved to decide whether they are the clowns or the monkeys in question.
2. A pandemic is merely a quantitative upgrade of an epidemic.
3. Philip Alcabes, *Dread How Fear and Fantasy Have Fueled Epidemics from the Black Death to Avian Flu*, PublicAffairs, New York, 2009.
4. It was already perfectly clear for Montaigne that men under stress are fools and fool themselves. Furthermore, that most of our current political leaders have been (in-)directly implicated in the process of dismantling public health care – something which proved fundamental, or better, fundamentally lacking in this health crisis – then one can easily understand the disastrous non-deciding and continuous contradicting that has characterized and is still characterizing these peculiar times.
5. Obviously, politicians never truly trust their constituents and they constantly fear losing their vote, but this can never become an explicit, let alone institutional, aspect of democratic politics. It is the people (the *demos*) who have the power (*kratos*). The moment the *demos* is declared untrustworthy, we are no longer in a democracy.
6. Frank Furedi, *Culture of Fear: Risk Taking and the Morality of Low Expectation* , Cassell, London, 1997.
7. But if there is no reference possible to anything that we have previously experienced, why are all the political and, especially medical leaders, so certain about all they say?
8. Furthermore, considering that the biggest problem consisted of the availability of hospital beds and respiration equipment, the question should be raised as to why not a single country in the world has greatly invested in these resources to fight this virus.

Coming Out of the *Comfort Zone*, in Liturgy What Have We Learned?: New Possible Scenarios for Rites Tested by Lockdown

ALBERTO DAL MASO

From 21 February 2020 Italy, first among the Western nations, was forced to adopt drastic containment measures in response to a new coronavirus, both highly contagious and completely unknown to our immune system. Between 9 March and 3 May it was forbidden to leave one's house except for demonstrably essential reasons.[1] The abolition of the usual "civil rites" determined a new existential condition in which the structure of time seemed to be suspended. The ban on "religious rites", which caught everyone unprepared, plunged churches, mosques, and synagogues into an unknown and agonising dimension. The Italian Catholic Church, too, caught in a forest of restrictions right at the start of Lent, was exposed as fragile. Gripped by paralysing feelings of uncertainty, precariousness, and impotence it had to completely re-organise itself at a pastoral level. Thanks to the unanimous effort of modification, the enormous initial distress and disorientation were gradually tempered. Then the more perceptible and reactive voices began to read theologically the hard *stress test* to which, without let-up, they were being subjected. In biblical terms the Covid-19 pandemic appeared above all to be a *peirasmós*, a "trial"; but many people also identified in it an *apokálypsis*, a revelatory moment, a revelation, and at the same time a *kairós*, a unique opportunity for purification and conversion.

With regard to the liturgy, the public authorities' restrictive measures to contain the spread of infection brought a halt to customary practices and forced recourse to replacement forms of celebration. The liturgical life – fundamental to the very nature of the church – was not interrupted *tout-court*, but took place differently, re-located to other spaces, expressed in other languages. Faced with the prolonged eucharistic fast, parishes experienced or became protagonists of change, either dusting down ancient action plans, or allowing themselves to be transported by the wind of impetuous creativity. Everyone worked things out according to their own pre-understandings and sensitivities, in a random order, but the scope of trajectories which followed, varied though it is, can be summarised in the three outlines of reactions which we will now review.

I Officiating at a clerical mass "behind closed doors": inertia or regression?

The most instinctive reaction was that of bringing back into vogue mass "without the people". If every "not strictly individual ceremony" was forbidden and if worship is an imperative, then the only option open to priests was to resort to *their* mass, officiating behind closed doors. For centuries that was how things worked anyway, so why give up the reassuring warmth of the ancient custom? The rite was necessity and obligation, desire and honour: to celebrate it *anyway* allowed the fulfilment of a fitting act of eucharistic devotion (placating feelings of guilt) and seeing the satisfaction of identity demands (a need for recognition). The priest returned to being sole protagonist who, through a power only his, consecrated the bread and wine on the altar "on behalf of" the simple faithful, not authorised to participate.[2] In the solitary mass or mass for a few, he could exempt himself from presiding over a celebrating assembly and fool himself into replacing the community.[3] Under the pressure of the disease anachronistic conceptions of the eucharistic, conceptions of an antiquated aftertaste, re-emerged: a "small ancient world" reproduced itself as normal, taken for granted – that retroverted model of church whose misrepresentations Vatican II had tried to fix.

Is this resistance to the eucharistic fast to the bitter end reducible to simple flaws, to blunders dictated by the urgency to react? Does it attest to the essential nature of the mass for the church, to the point that the scandalous idea of the disappearance of the former would de facto mean the disappearance of the latter? Perhaps the majority did not intentionally desire to reject the Council or to decree that the beautiful principles of the liturgical reform are a luxury which, when things get hard, can no longer be allowed. But, good intentions apart, few seemed to have realised the resounding contradiction: a eucharistic act reduced to a clerical matter not only endorsed social distancing in the sacramental symbols, did not just render the intrinsic bond between eucharistic body and ecclesial body as pleonastic, but could hardly inaugurate *per ritus et preces* the demanding and vertiginous edification of the whole church in the unity of the body of Christ. The marked pre-conciliar flavour of this regressive option, entirely played out on a nostalgic terrain, is undeniable, at both the theological and the pastoral level.

And the faithful? As ideal *pendant* of this neo-Tridentine experience, a non-gathered people sought refuge in devotions. There was an increase in recourse to rosaries and kissing crucifixes, to the most imaginary chaplets and prayers before the tabernacle in the empty church – humble, direct, immediate expressions of a simple Christianity, with strong emotional emphases. Nor was there any lack of exaggeration with a spectacular impact, of hints of fideism or superstition or the miraculous; there was even the revival of a private form. For the official church it was easier to entertain these expressions of devotion, even encourage them, rather than force itself to substantiate them with evangelical breath, to lead them back to the paschal heart of worship, to raise them to a reading of ecclesial faith in the pandemic.

At this level Vatican II as a vision of a renewed understanding of spirituality, of liturgy, of eucharistic theology, of ecclesiology and of the ordained ministry revealed itself to be more of a stereotype than a solid reality. To have not grasped the premises implicit in these choices reveals how little the foundations of *Sacrosanctum concilium* are rooted in Italy, among the faithful and pastors. We have not left the Tridentine paradigm. A complete, not superficial reception of Vatican II is still a work in progress.

II Broadcasting "digital" masses: a realised future or unquestioning fascination?

The most *trendy* reaction was to replace mass in the presence of people with mass *live-streaming*. Today technology is a resource, so why not use it to enter people's houses? The *bricoleur* parish priest switched on the *tablet* and enthusiastically arranged himself for the *webcam*. So, alongside the usual service offered by Italian public TV was a plethora not just of local broadcasters, but above all *social* channels. The attempt was praiseworthy: to bridge a distance, testifying to the strength of the sacrament.

On the positive side, the variety of what was offered enabled part of the community to reach virtually their own pastor in the act of celebrating, rather than having to assist at a 'foreign' eucharist, or rather broadcast from "someone else's" church, 'somewhere else'. In extreme conditions of isolation, the aggregative strength of the digital – at a time when many of us live a double of one's life on the internet and the differences between virtual and real are becoming increasingly vague – understandably gave rise to almost miraculous expectations.

However, anxiety about fulfilling the Sunday obligation *online*, along with an inadequate critical awareness of the intertwining of the potential and the risks associated with modern *media*, gave rise to the emergence of a vast collection of limitations: careless improvisation, homiletic mediocrity, communicative incompetence, with embarrassing touches of folklore.[4] Certain compulsive reflections on the Mass as remote rather than pastoral impetus demonstrated a yearning for clerical visibility (since the other baptised were banished from the screens, too). And yet the digital rite was not able to fill the deserted liturgical space: it did not restore a nucleus of presence. In the virtual world one is "with" others, but "alone", each on their own: *Alone Together*, Sherry Turkle would say. Fluid objects, accessed by a click, these *prêt-à-porter* liturgies are available to everyone: it is the very *design* of the digital means which disconnects them from the community bond and exposes them to individual choice in the *mare magnum* of the internet's offering. Undemanding, they require a minimum level of involvement (not just in the somatic sense), even lower than the interaction demanded by a common videogame.[5] Anyone can

131

simultaneously 'participate' in Mass and cook, or chat with a friend, or do stretches: they are connected, but inevitably distracted.

In the specific case of the eucharistic celebration the real negative was something else: the virtual rite is disembodied, and so a vertiginous suppression of the very logics of the rite, which involve *as substantial* the experience of gaze and contact, of posture and gesture, of senses such as taste and smell. The mass transferred to the *smartphone* is an unacceptable internal division of the ecclesial subject, weakened in its wholeness (how many poor and elderly people do not have access to the new technologies?), split between exclusive actors and passive spectators (following the television scheme of mono-directional communication). Tending towards a sort of sacramental materialism, the "telegenic" eucharist is an unnatural abstraction of the epiclesis over the gifts from the epiclesis over the communicants – but to them access to communion in the one bread and one wine is forbidden. The virtualisation of the mass is a religious spectacle which, in the end, sees the eucharist deny itself as the original *mysterium* of the community, the expression-and-realisation of the unity in Christ of all the baptised. *Smart work* can exist, but it will never be able to provide a quick Mass, unless it distorts it to a simple subtitle.

In the end, rather than an amazing solution, recourse to the internet offered a surrogate, traversed by troubles and pitfalls. It was a shortcut, bearable as a temporary emergency measure. It is essential not to close one's eyes to the problems of the *medium* used and their implications.

III Celebrating, beyond *sola missa*, in the domestic churches: early glimmers

It was definitely necessary to think of something else. And so the third typology of reaction, the most mature, was that of the domestic liturgies on the Lord's day. The small family communities – tiny, virtuous, rather than viral *clusters* – were shielded by the health restrictions: they were able to continue to live in close contact, sharing meals and family gestures of affection. Here a not-enfeebled prayer and a discreet, inclusive celebration could take place – not being outside the world, but from within, not replacing the community, but valuing it (*empowering*) from its generative nucleus.

a) 'God dwelling in their homes, in their streets and squares' (EG 71)

Of course, we were completely helpless: lacking in previous experiences (the *domus ecclesiae* are very far back in time), in theoretical premises ("domestic celebration" seemed to be an oxymoron), in formation and practical "equipment". This is without taking into account that it is easier to listen to a mass on TV than celebrate in the family. However, some pioneers set to work with creativity, sharing the charisms of each, to actually organise rites which adopted the language of everyday life. And they achieved and spread ad hoc support which gave rise to simple and expressive liturgies, genuinely evangelical and pertinent to the narrative. This enlightened solution was developed for subsequent iterations: they had to redesign words, re-adapt gestures, rediscover spaces, prepare contexts, to invoke the Christ who draws close and saves, even in a time of abeyance and fear.

Driven by events, and among a thousand difficulties, we learned to recognise:

- the original potentiality of the Word, in its sacramentality (not as expedient or surrogate of the rite, and even less as a private act or solipsistic intellectual practice);
- the essence of the baptismal priesthood, in which it is the 'priestly community' of LG 11 celebrating (the former, unlike the ministerial priesthood, was not subject to hygiene restrictions);
- the ministeriality of the couple united in the sacrament of matrimony and its lay spirituality (without thereby discrediting single baptised individuals, people living together or de facto families);
- the house as a place of worship, as experience of church (beyond the empty and oversentimental rhetoric of the "domestic church"), at the time when people were forced to remain isolated, without ever being alone.

There was no reluctance to spend spending energy on stopgap measures which simulated normality. There was an acceptance of passing into the crucible of that strange liminal space-time which, in the suspension of the ordinary, was removed of the old certainties but harbinger of a initiatory journey. There was a void – the impossibility of an integral eucharist – and people became used to an absence which demanded being interpreted in rituality, to the point of anticipating a Presence not confined to the sacred vessels nor preserved in the *votum sacramenti*. It is about making real the 'Where two or three are gathered in my name, there I am in the midst of them ...' of Matt 18:20, involving the entire people of God, from the base, with new and differentiated ways of participating, which were within their reach: prayers expert in humanity, reflections and meditations accompanied by simple gestures, comments on the Word, liturgies re-adapted to the context.[6]

Realistically, the change was abrupt. Single people, married couples, parents, families were not always thinking about the suggestions of domestic prayer. If steering the moments of family worship was difficult for people accustomed to practising, it was very hard for less assiduous faithful or for those, conversely, more attached to the traditions. After the idealizations, they were modest, basic liturgies imbued with the workaday. Nevertheless they embodied an ideal to strive for asymptotically in the post-pandemic era, too. Not because the domestic celebration (which extends well beyond "saying prayers") must replace the parish celebration (which extends well beyond the domestic walls), but because the latter know how to involve dimensions – such as profound adherence to the familiar daily life, the universal priesthood of the faithful – which it is hard to take. The two moments have a different nature and different perspectives, and are seen as distinct and allied, not as replacement and adversary, in a manner in which they can indeed mutually feed and tarnish each other in the frequenting of the one Mystery.

b) A plurality of liturgical expressions to be reconsidered
At the heart of the celebratory domestic-family dynamic is an intuition: to give dignity to a plurality of liturgical expressions, capable of enabling 'the exercise of the priestly office of Jesus Christ' (SC 7) in the church. Between the "maximum" of the eucharist celebration and the "minimum" of a meagre implicit prayer there can and must exist a whole range of intermediary forms of liturgical life.[7]

Among the other critical issues of the pre-Covid era there emerged the Mass as obligated-and-assumed gesture, as clerical automatism, as obsessive "tic", as an almost unique form of Christian rituality, rather than its summit (*culmen*, arrival point for a long communal journey, not just *fons*). In the course of time the eucharist, 'tasteless unleavened bread of parallel customs and lives' (François Cassingena-Trévedy), 'sign of a wooden, stuck community' (Luigi Sartori), pervasive rite inflated by routine, serially multiplied, surpassed all the other elements of a Christian liturgical life, to the point that without the Mass they seemed to have no dignity.

The restrictions to stop the pandemic helped the reassessment of the *loghiké latréia* of Rom 12:1. And, in this perspective, they highlighted the need to

- benefit from the most serene celebratory languages and styles, more substantial than the ordinary, which intercept lived experience and bring it within the rite;
- rediscover the anthropological background of belief and celebration, in other words the "extra-ritual part" not just of the eucharist, but also of reconciliation, of the ministry of consoling those in mourning, of caring for those experiencing illness;
- recognise the potentiality of two pillars of the Catholic liturgical edifice as the liturgy of the Word and the liturgy of the Hours,[9] and also realise new "intermediary" celebratory forms similar to those;
- "unpack" the eucharist in the individual ritual sequences which comprise it, savouring them individually.[9]

And this, not out of a habit of disintermediation, but out of a more lively view of the subject of Christian worship (Christ who unites to himself the whole church, not just a part of it) and its contribution. And of course all this in a relation of give-and-take with the heptasyllabic sacramental body.

IV Will nothing be the same as before? The duty to discern and ... recreate

The pandemic, forcing us to abandon the reassuring *comfort zone*, has revealed resistance, shortcomings, and inconsistencies, and has helped to re-focus on the essential. Once the emergency has returned, will we just return to the known assets, condemning us to forget?

135

The trial we have undergone, that of a eucharist taken away, gave us tangible changes which, on more fronts, imply a deconstruction. It called on us to achieve a truly multiform liturgy, yet reconsidering, according to criteria of frugality, the *quantity* of sacramental actions we celebrate, which are not the whole of the ecclesial event and are not isolated from the other community dynamics, even before it called on us to monitor the *quality* of things and gestures, of words and relations which substantiate the liturgy – and to monitor their truth! It called on us to guarantee a mutual osmosis between the language of the rite and the drama of life: liturgical services stripped of an empty pomposity must be able to promise an intense symbolisation and be significant for the human condition, giving it meaning. It called on us to recover the whole church for the liturgy, going beyond the monopoly of some, the church realised as celebrating subject: "All the baptised are priests" must change from nominal affirmation to substantial truth. It asked us to observe the festive obligation from another perspective, without focussing in a restrictive and monotonous way on the *dominicum* on just the eucharistic celebration, but broadening the outlook to those attitudes which substantiate 'the encounter without which we cannot live'.[10] Are we able to undertake any discernment about these entreaties and authoritative pleas?

But the previously unknown and agonising situation of Covid-19, while it shook us profoundly as individuals and as church (as well as society) also planted invisible changes. Fundamentally, it matured, sharpened, increased our perception, making us dream of an overall reorganisation: not just savouring more spacious individual practices or more dynamic structures, but desiring a new style.

In his 2012 *Recomposed*, Max Richter re-codified in a radically contemporary language – with a sincere and meticulous integral re-writing – Antonio Vivaldi's most famous work, milestone of the late Italian baroque: *The Four Seasons*. Similarly, we, too, have to recreate: rediscover, re-interpret, re-contextualise the legacy tradition has entrusted to us and embed it into the contemporary spiritual landscape. That is, to take up again the impulse of the last Council, restart a process; to give meaning again to the classic languages, translating them into new forms and transposing their meaning, synchronised with a more vital and broader human reality, to the extent of making everyone fall in love with it again, but without ever falling into the trap of taming the Mystery. Do we know how to courageously enhance the experience of this such demanding trial, demonstrating that it has not been experienced in vain?

Translated by Patricia and Liam Kelly

Notes

1. This text focuses on the so-called "Phase 1" of the pandemic, the period marked by *lockdown* measures, and does not consider what emerged at a liturgical level in "Phase 2", consisting in a partial relaxation of those measures.
2. The collective nature of the pandemic threat has not cancelled the disparity of *duo genera christianorum*: in fact, this worn-out paraphernalia was strongly reaffirmed not just by a eucharistic synaxis reduced to the "sacred duty of the priest", but also by the scarce or non-existent involvement of members of the laity of the various church councils of the decision-making processes to tackle Phase 1 (*cf.* A. Join-Lambert, 'Leçons du confinement pour l'Église', in *Études* 4275 [2020] 79-90, (86)).
3. If a priest, finally free from the distractions and interferences represented by the liturgical assemblies and/or brothers, were able to say that he was pleased at a rediscovered "spiritual intimacy with Divine Teacher", a certain number of ordained ministers – this exception should be noted – have chosen not to live their own status as a privilege (or an "Everyman for himself") and, albeit in a painful way, have prefered to share the eucharistic fast with their own community, out of a sense of solidarity, by not presiding at solitary masses.
4. Some performances, worthy of the apprentice Disney witch of *Fantasia* (1940), almost lead to justifying the bishops who jealousy kept to themselves the exclusive faculty of broadcasting the Sunday rites.
5. Which paradoxically succeeded in bringing closer some who were "distant" – like some young people, caught between belief and incredulity – who were previously immune to the demanding community rite.
6. It was about 'rediscovering the relationship with the paschal mystery, as it happens in the heard Word, in rythmical prayer and in meditated penance', so in 'rites which are not necessary, which change styles and languages, bodies and hearts'. A Grillo, 'La nostalgia e il desiderio della liturgia', in *Rivista di pastorale liturgica* special edition. (March 2020) 4-8, (8). *Cf.* Also G. Grandi, 'La liturgia alla prova del "digiuno eucaristico"', in L. Alici, G. DeSimone, and P. Grassi (eds.), *La fede e il contagio. Nel tempo della pandemia*, Ave, Rome 2020, 58-60.
7. Andrea Grillo appeals to 'an articulate experience of levels and limits of an experience of prayer and celebration. Precisely this articulation would enable a different play of subjects, of ministers, places and responsibilities', respecting 'a necessary differentiation of manners, places and times' (Grillo, 'La nostalgia e il desiderio della liturgia', 7).
8. Both seem more compatible with transfer to digital platforms such as zoom or skype which enable inter-action and exchange in small gropups (although at the price of restricting the purely gestural dimension).
9. The Mass, with its 'wealth of elements', regularly sees them "packaged" according to a fixed scheme; instead it would be desirable 'at least every so often to peel away the parts to

experience each independently: one thinks of independent celebrations of the word of God, of penance, of prayer, of adoration, of critical reflection on the facts of the day, the mutual exercise of fraternal correction, of exhortation, that is Christian prophecy, the sending to mission of all the services and ministries for dedication in daily life…'; thus wrote L. Sartori in less suspect times; 'Premesse teologiche per un discorso sui ministeri ecclesiali', in *Humanitas* 33/12 (1978) 9-20, (19f).

10. M. Magoni, 'La domenica non andando alla messa', in *Rivista di pastorale liturgica* special edition (June 2020) 17-19 (19); *cf.* also M. Semeraro,' Il clericalismo è guarito?', in *Rivista di pastorale liturgica* special edition (June 2020), 35-37. In a certain sense it is also foreseen by canon 1248, § 2.

Contributors

ANNA STAROPOLI is a Sociologist at the Institute of Political Training "Pedro Arrupe" in Palermo, with experience in research and action on marginality, active citizenship and social policies. She is pedagogical tutor in the research paths "Idea-Action" of the Arrupe Institute and in the academic course of the Institute of Religious Sciences at the Theological Faculty of Sicily. She collaborates with the O.U. of Mediations and Reparatory Justice of the Municipality of Palermo, the Don Calabria Institute, the Waldensian Institute and the Spondè Association for the activity of Community Mediation of Conflicts. It is in the coordination of the National Forum of Civil Ethics. She is the regional contact person for Sicily of JSN for actions against poverty. She is vice-director of the Social Pastoral and Labour Office of the Diocese of Palermo.

Address: Via Paolo Amato, n.15 90138 Palermo, Italy

Email: anna.staropoli@istitutoarrupe.it

SHARON A. BONG is Associate Professor of Gender Studies at the School of Arts and Social Sciences, Monash University Malaysia. She graduated with a Ph.D. in Religious Studies (2002) and M.A. in Women and Religion (1997), University of Lancaster, UK. She has authored *Becoming queer and religious in Malaysia and Singapore* (2020), *The Tension Between Women's Rights and Religions: The Case of Malaysia* (2006) and edited *Trauma, Memory and Transformation in Southeast Asia* (2014) and *Re-imagining Marriage and Family in Asia: Asian Christian Women's Perspectives* (2008). She is currently consultant to and former coordinator of the Ecclesia of Women in Asia, a forum writer for the Catholic Theological Ethics in the World Church and member of the Concilium Board of Editors.

Address: Associate Prof. Dr. Sharon A. Bong, School of Arts & Social Sciences, Monash University Malaysia, Jalan Lagoon Selatan, 47500

Bandar Sunway, Selangor Darul Ehsan, Malaysia
Email: Sharon.bong@monash.edu

CARLOS MENDOZA-ÁLVAREZ OP - Mexican Dominican, researcher in fundamental theology with a post-modern and decolonial perspective. He has been a member of the Mexican National Researchers System since 2002. He is a full-time academic at the Universidad Iberoamericana in Mexico City and a visiting professor at Boston College. He has written a trilogy on the idea of revelation: Deus liberans (Fribourg, 1996), Deus absconditus (Paris, 2011, in French) and Deus ineffabilis (Barcelona, 2015). He has started a new trilogy on the idea of tradition of which the first volume is *La resurrección como anticipación mesiánica. Duelo, memoria y esperanza desde los sobrevivientes* (Mexico City, 2020).

Address: Universidad Iberoamericana Ciudad de México, Prol. Paseo de la Reforma 880, Lomas de Santa Fe, Delegación Cuajimalpa, 01219 México, D.F., Mexico
Email: carlos.mendoza@ibero.mx

GIOVANNI GIORGIO - The author was professor in Theoretical Philosophy at Rome's Pontifical Lateran University and at the Abruzzese-Molisano Theological Institute in Chieti, where he was Dean from 2006 to 2010. In the same period he was director of the Rome journal Ricerche teologiche. From 2003 until 2008 he was editorial coordinator of the journal Prospettiva persona in Teramo, a work of the Research Centre on Personalism based in the same city. As well as articles and contributions on the themes of hermeneutics, philosophical anthropology, and general ethics in journals and edited works, he has edited the publication of works of a theological nature, including: (ed.) *Gianni Vattimo, Carmelo Dotolo, Dio: la possibilità buona. Un colloquio sulla soglia tra filosofia e teologia, Rubbettino, Soveria Mannelli, 2009 [translated into Spanish in 2012]*. Recent works of a philosophical nature include: Cyborg: Il volto dell'uomo futuro. Il postumano fra natura e cultura, Cittadella, Assisi 2017.

Address: Via Cona 106 – 64100 Teramo, Italy
E-mail: giovannigiorgio61@gmail.com

STAN CHU ILO is a research professor of World Christianity and African Studies at the Centre for World Catholicism and Intercultural Theology, DePaul University, Chicago, USA; and the Coordinator of the Pan-African Catholic Theology and Pastoral Network; and honorary professor of theology and religion at Durham University, Durham, England. His latest book is, *Someone Beautiful to God: Finding the Light of Faith in a Wounded World* (2020).

Address: Prof. Dr. Stan Chu Ilo, 020 N. 76th Court, Elmwood Park, IL 60707, USA
Email: silo@depaul.edu

MICHELLE BECKA is a theologian and professor of Christian social ethics. She gained her doctoral degree in 2004 with a thesis of interculturality and recognition and her professorial degree in 2014 in Mainz with a dissertation on 'Ethics in the administration of justice'. Since 2016 she has been professor of Christian social ethics at the university of Würzburg. The main focuses of her research are the principles of social ethics, ethics in the administration of justice, migration and ethics, ethics and human rights, interculturality, etc.

Address: Prof. Dr. Michelle Becka, Universität Würzburg, Fakultät für Katholische Theologie, Bibrastraße 14, 97070 Würzburg, Germany
Email: michelle.becka@uni-wuerzburg.de

JOHANNES ULRICH BA has studied theology and philosophy. He is a student of humane medicine and an academic assistant at the Chair of Christian social ethics at the university of Würzburg. His academic writing to date has been in the field of ethics and on the molecular biology of *Echinococcus multilocularis*.

Address: Johannes Ulrich, c/o Richard Ulrich, Bühringerstraße 20, 91710 Gunzenhausen, Germany
Email: johannes.ulrich@googlemail.com

Publications of Becka and Ulrich: Becka and Ulrich, *Ethik im Vollzug. Handreichung für die ethische Fallreflexion*, Münster 2020; Becka and Ulrich, 'Blinde Praxis, taube Theorie? Sozialethische Reflexion über das Menschenrecht auf Gesundheit', in: Bernhard Emunds, (ed.) *Christliche*

Sozialethik – Orientierung welcher Praxis?, Stuttgart, 301-321.

CETTINA MILITELLO Ph.D., STh.D., a lay person, began teaching in Sicily's Faculty of Theology (Palermo) in 1975. She then became a permanent lecturer at the Pontifical Liturgical Institute (Rome) and a guest lecturer in other academic Centres. She is currently Director of the "Costanza Scelfo Institute for the problems of the laity and women in the Church" (Department of SIRT) and holds the "Women and Christianity" Chair at the Pontifical "Marianum" Faculty of Theology. Her academic interests are focussed on ecclesiology, Mariology, women in the Church, and the relationship between ecclesiology and liturgy. Her publications include *La Chiesa "il Corpo Crismato"*, EDB, Bologna 2013 (reprinted) and, recently, *Le donne e la riforma della Chiesa* (with S. Noceti), EDB, Bologna 2017; *Vi è stato detto, ma io vi dico. Una rilettura dei 10 comandamenti*, San Paolo, Cinisello B. 2018; *Maria con occhi di donna. Nuovi Saggi*, San Paolo, Cinisello B. 2019; *Ripensare il Ministero. Necessità e sfida per la Chiesa*, Nerbini, Florence 2019.

Address: C/o Pontificia Facoltà Teologica "Marianum", Viale Trenta Aprile n.6 – 00153, Rome, Italy
Email: teologa45@gmail.com

ZORAN GROZDANOV, Assistant Professor at the University Centre for Protestant Theology Matthias Flacius Illyricus, University in Zagreb. He has recently co-edited the *Envisioning the Good Life* volume, in honor of Miroslav Volf (Wipf&Stock, Oregon, 2017), and *Balkan Contextual Theology* (Routledge, London-New York, to be published), with Stipe Odak. Grozdanov has also published several articles on the relationship of ethnic, national, and religious belonging in former Yugoslavia.

Address: University Centre for Protestant Theology MFI, Ivana Lučića 1a, HR-10000 Zagreb, Croatia
Email: zoran.grozdanov@tfmvi.hr

VALERIO CORRADI, holds a Ph.D. in the Sociology and Methodology of social research and teaches geographical sociology at the Catholic University Sacro Cuore, and works with Brescia's Centre of Initiatives and Research on Migration (CIRMiB) and with the Centre for International

Studies into Geopolitics (Ce.St.In.Geo.).
Address: Via Trieste, 17 25121 - Brescia; Italy
Email: valerio.corradi@unicatt.it

GIUSEPPINA DE SIMONE is Professor in the Philosophy of Religion and co-ordinator of the Specialisation in Fundamental Theology – Theology of Religious Experience in the Mediterranean context at the Pontifical Theological Faculty of Southern Italy – San Luigi Section (Naples). She is also a lecturer at the Pontifical Lateran University and director of the journal *Dialoghi*. She is a member of the Executive Committee of the Italian Association of the Philosophy of Religion. Her studies are based on philosophy and theology and in particular religious experience, the affective roots of knowledge, the speculative significance of Christian revelation and faith experience. An academic in contemporary phenomenology, she edited the Italian translation of M. Henry, *L'essenza della manifestazione*, Orthotes, Salerno-Naples 2018. She was part of the systematic committee which prepared the meeting of reflection and prayer of the Bishops of the Mediterranean, *Mediterranean frontier of peace* (Bari 19-23 February 2020) and gave the introductory address on 20 February on the theme 'Handing on faith to future generations. The Mediterranean's challenges and resources'.
Address: Via Ercole Cantone 122, 80038 Pomigliano d'Arco (Na), Italy
Email: desimone.giuseppina@gmail.com

CRISPINO VALENZIANO studied in Rome at the Pontifical Gregorian University and in Genoa at the State University. He specialized at the University of Strasbourg and at the Sorbonne in Paris. He has worked with professors M. Nédoncelle, M.F. Sciacca, C.L. Strauss. He is full professor at the Pontifical Liturgical Institute of the Anselmian Athenaeum in Rome. His teaching and research are in the areas of Liturgy, Anthropology, Culture and Art. He focuses on the questions and problems of proximity and intersection between the theological and human sciences, focusing on mystagogy and pastoral theology, cultural studies and ecclesial biology. He is an Honorary Doctor of Pontifical and State Universities, in Theology, Liturgy and Architecture. In response to Vatican II and the implementation of its innovative requests, he is committed to promoting

theology in via pulchritudinis. His latest work is *The Crucifix of Francis of Assisi*, Antonianum, Rome 2020.
  Address: Viale Cavour n. 26 – 90015 Cefalù, Palermo, Itay
  Email c.militello@virgilio.it

KRISTOF K.P. VANHOUTTE is Core Faculty at the Paris Institute for Critical Thinking and a Research Fellow at the Department of Philosophy of the University of the Free State. Kristof has published on topics in continental philosophy, philosophy of literature, patristics, theology-philosophy-politics interdependencies, educational theory, and soccer. His latest book is *Limbo Reapplied. On Living in Perennial Crisis and the Immanent Afterlife* (Palgrave Macmillan 2018).
  Address: Schützenmattstrasse 9, 4051 Basel, Switzerland
  Email: vanhkristof@hotmail.com

ALBERTO DAL MASO A married man and father of two, he gained his doctorate in theology at Padua's "S. Giustina" Institute of Pastoral Liturgy. He taught Pastoral Liturgy and Liturgy and communication at Rome's Pontifical Lateran University, as well as History and forms of Christian worship at the Bruno Kessler Foundation's Higher Course of Religious Sciences in Trento. Since 1998 he has been working at the publishers Editrice Queriniana in Brescia, where, *inter alia*, he is the editor responsible for the Italian edition of *Concilium*. His publications include *L'efficacia dei sacramenti e la performance rituale. Ripensare l'«ex opere operato» a partire dall'antropologia culturale* (Padua 1999) and *Prometto di amarti e onorarti. Per preparare e celebrare la messa degli sposi* (Brescia 2004).
  Address: Alberto Dal Maso, via Antonio Vivaldi 2, I-37044 Cologna Veneta, Verona, Italy
  Email: a_dalmaso@email.it

HYMNS **Ancient & Modern**

The Canterbury Dictionary of HYMNOLOGY

The result of over ten years of research by an international team of editors, The Canterbury Dictionary of Hymnology is the major online reference work on hymns, hymn-writers and traditions.

www.hymnology.co.uk

CHURCH TIMES

The Church Times, founded in 1863, has become the world's leading Anglican newspaper. It offers professional reporting of UK and international church news, in-depth features on faith, arts and culture, wide-ranging comment and all the latest clergy jobs. Available in print and online.

www.churchtimes.co.uk

Crucible

Crucible is the Christian journal of social ethics. It is produced quarterly, pulling together some of the best practitioners, thinkers, and theologians in the field. Each issue reflects theologically on a key theme of political, social, cultural, or environmental significance.

www.cruciblejournal.co.uk

JLS

Joint Liturgical Studies offers a valuable contribution to the study of liturgy. Each issue considers a particular aspect of liturgical development, such as the origins of the Roman rite, Anglican Orders, welcoming the Baptised, and Anglican Missals.

www.jointliturgicalstudies.co.uk

magnet

Magnet is a resource magazine published three times a year. Packed with ideas for worship, inspiring artwork and stories of faith and justice from around the world.

www.ourmagnet.co.uk

For more information on these publications visit the websites listed above or contact **Hymns Ancient & Modern:**
Tel.: +44 (0)1603 785 910
Write to: Subscriptions, Hymns Ancient & Modern,
13a Hellesdon Park Road, Norwich NR6 5DR

Concilium Subscription Information

April	**2021/2:** *Sinodality*
July	**2021/3:** *Incarnation*
October	**2021/4:** *Amazons/Congo*
December	**2021/5:** *End of Life*
February	**2022/1:** *Theology in Asia*

New subscribers: to receive the next five issues of Concilium please copy this form, complete it in block capitals and send it with your payment to the address below. Alternatively subscribe online at www.conciliumjournal.co.uk

Please enter my annual subscription for Concilium starting with issue 2021/2.

Individuals
____ £52 UK
____ £75 overseas and (Euro €92, US $110)

Institutions
____ £75 UK
____ £95 overseas and (Euro €120, US $145)

Postage included – airmail for overseas subscribers

Payment Details:
Payment can be made by cheque or credit card.
a. I enclose a cheque for £/$/€ _____ Payable to Hymns Ancient and Modern Ltd
b. To pay by Visa/Mastercard please contact us on +44(0)1603 785911 or go to www.conciliumjournal.co.uk

Contact Details:
Name ....
Address ....
....
Telephone .... E-mail ....

Send your order to *Concilium*, **Hymns Ancient and Modern Ltd**
13a Hellesdon Park Road, Norwich NR6 5DR, UK
E-mail: concilium@hymnsam.co.uk
or order online at www.conciliumjournal.co.uk

Customer service information
All orders must be prepaid. Your subscription will begin with the next issue of Concilium. If you have any queries or require Information about other payment methods, please contact our Customer Services department.